Glen Burnie H. S. Media Center

AMERICA IN THE 20TH CENTURY

1960-1969

AMERICA IN THE 20TH CENTURY

SECOND EDITION
Revised and Expanded with Primary Sources

1960-1969

David Wright

Glen Burnie H. S. Media Center

MARSHALL CAVENDISH
NEW YORK • LONDON • TORONTO • SYDNEY

Marshall Cavendish
99 White Plains Road
Tarrytown, NY 10591

Website: www.marshallcavendish.com

© 1995, 2003 Marshall Cavendish Corporation

All rights reserved. No part of this book may be reproduced or utilized in any form or by any means electronic or mechanical including photocopying, recording or by any information storage and retrieval system, without permission of the copyright holders.

Library of Congress Cataloging-in-Publication Data

America in the 20th Century.-- 2nd ed., rev. and expanded with primary sources.
p. cm.
Includes bibliographical references and index.
ISBN 0-7614-7364-5 (set)
1. United States -- Civilization -- 20th century. I. Title: America in the twentieth century.
E169.1.A471872 2003
973.9--dc21

2001052949

ISBN 0-7614-7371-8 (vol. 7)

Printed in Malaysia
Bound in the United States of America

06 05 04 03 02 5 4 3 2 1

Series created by Discovery Books

Series Editor: Paul Humphrey
Academic Consultant: Gregory Bush,
Chair of History Department, University of Miami, Coral Gables
Marshall Cavendish Editor: Peter Mavrikis
Marshall Cavendish Production Manager: Alan Tsai
Project Editors: Valerie Weber and Yvonne Rees
Picture Research: Gillian Humphrey
Design Concept: Laurie Shock
Designers: Ian Winton and Winsome Malcolm

(Frontispiece) The Apollo 11 lunar module Eagle, *with astronauts Neil Armstrong and Edwin Aldrin aboard, photographed from the command module during a rendezvous in lunar orbit on July 21, 1969.*

Contents

CHAPTER 1
A Decade Unfolds

"The torch has been passed to a new generation of Americans — born in this century, tempered by war, disciplined by a hard and bitter peace, proud of our ancient heritage — and unwilling to witness or permit the slow undoing of those human rights to which this nation is committed, and to which we are committed today at home and around the world."

A typical all-American, fifties suburban lifestyle is depicted in this advertisement for Maxwell House coffee, 1950. The traditional female stereotype was a strong advertising symbol, then as now.

The words of President John F. Kennedy in his 1961 inauguration speech, hailed by Republicans and Democrats alike as one of the best in memory, are an apt preface to a decade marked by momentous social, political, and technological events and achievements. It was also to suffer the continuing threat of nuclear war, the spread of communism in Southeast Asia — and much closer to home on the island of Cuba, growing discontent among African-Americans, and the traumas of a youth coming to grips with its own identity.

During the 1950s, few Americans questioned the social order of the time. Some critics, such as Jack Kerouac and Allen Ginsberg, turned away from the prevalent social and cultural values, but most were content with the status quo. Eisenhower's presidency reflected this view. He adopted middle-of-the-road policies and consensus decision-making and proved popular. As one columnist noted in 1959, "The public loves Ike. The less he does, the more they love him. That probably is the secret. Here is a man who doesn't rock the boat."

By the 1960s, however, many young Americans were looking for something more. They began to seriously question the attitudes of their parents and their politicians. To many, Jack Kennedy seemed an embodiment of their hopes and aspirations for the future.

But just three days before Kennedy made his inaugural speech, the retiring president Eisenhower startled people in the capital when his farewell speech, expected by most to be soft and sentimental, instead warned the American people against "the acquisition of unwarranted influence by the military-industrial complex," and to guard their liberties from a "conjunction of an immense military establishment and a large arms industry."

What Eisenhower feared most was that the massive buildup of conventional and nuclear arms and the huge industries that had grown to fuel the arms race would exert unwarranted influence on the destiny of the American people. He concluded his speech with a prayer that "all peoples will come together in peace guaranteed by mutual respect and love." The events that unfolded during one of the most tumultuous decades of this century were in many respects quite the reverse.

A Backward Glance

An American looking backward from January 1, 1960, could see great events that were to influence the decade ahead. They included:

- *World War II.* Lasting six years in Europe and longer in East Asia, the conflict ended in 1945 with North America untouched and owner of the world's largest and most productive industries. The United States tried war criminals, spent $12 billion helping friends and former enemies rebuild their countries, and helped create boundaries for several new, postwar nations. The government also looked after its own. The unprecedented GI Bill of Rights was signed into law in 1944 to help returning veterans obtain money for additional education and low-cost home mortgages. This led to a huge demand for housing after the war and to a construction boom that fostered a trend towards mass-production and standardization in house design and construction. In all, thirteen million new homes were built during the 1950s.

• *The baby boom.* As well as homes, many of those freshly discharged soldiers wanted cars and families. Beginning in 1945, large numbers of recently married couples began having children. The nation's population increased by 19 million during the 1940s and by 30 million in the 1950s in the postwar "baby boom" that continued right up to the sixties. In the fifties Americans married younger and had more children than their parents. Between 1940 and 1960, the birth rate of third children doubled and that of fourth children tripled.

New parents felt secure because the United States seemed a prosperous and safe place in which to live. One reason for such optimism was that minorities and others without economic power had not yet made their presence felt in any significant way countrywide. The arms and materials buildup leading to World War II had ended the Great Depression, and no one wanted to hear or read about being down and out anymore.

• *Civil, labor, and human rights.* Race riots ripped through Detroit in 1943, killing thirty-four and injuring seven hundred. A riot in the Harlem section of New York City that same year killed six people. Earlier, in 1940, novelist Richard Wright let whites know about black resentment with the publication of *Native Son*, the searing story of a young black male's crimes and the part society played in those crimes.

However, although the NAACP had increased its membership to 450,000 by 1946, they continued to employ strictly noncontroversial and nonviolent strategies to make their point — applying political pressure, taking legal action and educating African-Americans so they could help

"The law may not be able to make a man love me, but it can keep him from lynching me."

Martin Luther King, Jr.
1961

A mother and her five children living in a tent in Tennessee, 1961. "Tent cities" like these were set up for evicted sharecroppers and their families where they became part of the "invisible poor" — rural and urban families living in poverty that many prosperous Americans preferred to pretend did not exist. Author Michael Harrington writing in The Other America, *published in 1962, estimated that there were 50 million such "invisible" Americans.*

themselves. The picture was changing and it was clear that the days of overt subjugation of blacks were numbered.

Following the war, coal miners, railroad workers, and other laborers staged dramatic strikes for better wages and benefits. These were all unpleasant reminders that not every American was white, well-off, and moving forward.

- *The atomic bomb.* Scientist Albert Einstein told President Franklin D. Roosevelt of the bomb's awful potential in 1939. A grim, top-secret race took place between the United States and Nazi Germany throughout the war to see which nation would build the first atomic bomb. Roosevelt died on April 12, 1945, and Germany surrendered less than one month later as the war continued against Japan. Harry S. Truman, Roosevelt's successor, approved dropping atomic bombs on the busy Japanese cities of Hiroshima and Nagasaki. The Japanese surrendered on August 15, 1945, just six days after the second bomb fell, spreading death in a molten flash of light and heat. In all, 80,000 were killed instantly in Hiroshima and another 100,000 died later from burns, radiation, or other wounds from the blast. The Nagasaki bomb killed another 40,000.

- *The advance of communism.* The Soviet Union forced its form of government on eastern Europe, and Communists won control of China by 1949. In later years, throughout Africa, Asia, and South America, rebels such as Cuba's Fidel Castro saw communism as a way to achieve independence. These guerrillas often were armed by Communist nations. They faced governments frequently aided by the United States. One such war began in 1950 in Korea, near Japan. Communist North Koreans invaded the noncommunist south. The conflict was poorly understood by most people in the United States. Nevertheless, most citizens supported their country and the United Nations' military and economic aid without question. The war ended in a bloody standoff in 1953, with 54,246 Americans dead.

A Seedbed for the Sixties

These and other dramatic events began within five years of the end of World War II. Today, they overshadow the 1950s, a decade marked on one hand by faith in the United States' present and future and on the other by fears of a nuclear showdown. The 1950s seem at first glance to be boringly uneventful. But seeds planted from 1950 through 1959, a time *The World Almanac* labels "The American Decade," brought flowers that bloomed or wilted dramatically in the 1960s.

Eisenhower was president in the years between 1952 to 1960. He created a Department of Health, Education, and Welfare, extended the social security system and increased unemployment compensation to bring more people into the welfare safety net. He increased the hourly minimum wage from 75¢ to $1 and authorized the federal funding of housing for low income families. But, aside from these programs, his two terms in office were marked by a general lack of action within the country. Political commentators often criticized his consensus approach to decision-making as cumbersome and frequently ineffective.

That was not the case abroad. John Foster Dulles, Eisenhower's secretary of state, threatened to cut off aid to any nation even thinking about communism. The Eisenhower administration offered arms and money to Middle Eastern nations fighting Communist takeovers. How long could the country spend millions on containing communism?

China, Korea, and Southeast Asia were President Eisenhower's big concerns in Asia. In 1954, he refused to aid French troops surrounded by Communists in mountainous northern Vietnam, a small country south of China that France had begun to colonize and develop between 1860 and 1893. The defeated French were forced to leave the country. A truce created separate nations, Communist North Vietnam and noncommunist South Vietnam, plus Cambodia and Laos. The Eisenhower administration pinned its hopes in South Vietnam on a puppet president, Ngo Dinh Diem, who was a nationalist and fierce anticommunist. Between 1954 and 1961, the United States pumped over $1 billion into South Vietnam. Four dollars out of every five went to the military. The remainder was used to develop the South Vietnamese economy. But to most Americans, South Vietnam was a small country on the other side of the world. They looked at the new map of Southeast Asia and promptly forgot all about it.

More widely noticed was the space race. The world awoke one day in October 1957 to learn that the Soviet Union had fired a satellite called *Sputnik* into orbit around the earth. A U.S. satellite, *Explorer I*, orbited the earth in January 1958. Yet the work of the Soviets caused fear and unrest. Many Americans began to feel threatened by possible Soviet nuclear missiles. If they were first into space, could they also start — and win — a nuclear war? Was America complacent? Had the technological standards slipped that helped win World War II? Who was to blame? These feelings fed a space race spurred by fear and the desire to regain national pride in American technology.

Communism badly frightened many Americans, and a wave of anticommunism swept the country during the late 1940s and early 1950s. People began looking for Soviet spies all around them. The House Un-American Affairs Committee, or HUAC, held hearings that loudly declared the existence of Communists in the Truman administration. Then, in 1953, U.S. Senator Joseph McCarthy became chairman of the Senate subcommittee on investigations. McCarthy saw Communist spies and sympathizers everywhere. He and his associates ruined the careers of people inside and outside government, usually because these people had simply donated to pro-Communist causes or, years before, attended meetings. McCarthy was censured in 1954 for his heavy-handed tactics, but fear of communism became part of the Cold War. Schoolchildren across the United States were taught to prepare for nuclear attack. While some parents built backyard fallout shelters, local governments stashed food, medicine, and supplies should the Cold War turn hot.

The big winners of the Cold War were the defense contractors. Although the Eisenhower administration tried to control defense growth and keep down spending, the U.S.

Duck and cover disaster drills were commonplace for schoolchildren throughout the fifties and sixties when fears of communism and of nuclear attack were prevalent.

Navy and Air Force grew at rapid rates. It was in finally taking note of the many expensive weapons, and of far-flung land and sea bases, that Eisenhower warned of the power of "the military-industrial complex," the intimate working relationship between big defense contractors and the defense department. The former general's message would be taken to heart by the next generation.

Integrating Schools

Events in 1957 in Little Rock, Arkansas, would also make their mark. The U.S. Supreme Court had ruled in 1954, in the landmark *Brown v. the Board of Education of Topeka, Kansas,* decision, that segregation in public institutions was wrong and that equal amounts of money should be spent on all schoolchildren, regardless of race. The first test of the ruling was in Little Rock, where nine black high school students attempted to attend an all-white school. When the students were sent home to prevent violence, Eisenhower called out the National Guard to enforce court-ordered integration and allow the students to go to school.

The result of the Brown decision

African-American students escorted to high school by federal troops, Little Rock, Arkansas in 1957. The Supreme Court had ruled against segregation in public places in 1954, but in this case, President Eisenhower was compelled to use the National Guard to enforce the order.

"We don't expect to live in [these houses]... very long. Some of the junior executives expect to become seniors... and a lot of us will be transferred all over the U.S. .... We want to be sure there is a good resale value."

Couple agitating against black occupancy, Deerfield, Illinois, 1960

was massive white resistance to integration in previously segregated schools across the South. Opinion polls showed that 80 percent of southern whites opposed the Brown decision. Many white pupils, encouraged by their parents, refused to attend the integrated schools. In 1956, black student Autherine Lucy was suspended and then expelled from the University of Alabama following rioting by whites. The Ku Klux Klan re-emerged, while many less militant southerners joined White Citizens' Councils.

Eisenhower tried to adopt a neutral stance toward desegregation, both out of personal conviction and out of deference to his southern constituents. In 1957, however, he signed into law a civil rights bill that did away with many of the obstacles to black voters.

Television cameras covered school and public integration and the voting process. For many viewers outside the South, such coverage was a revelation. Footage of African-Americans being needlessly beaten and otherwise abused created a wave of sympathy among many of the white citizens.

If more and more white people backed black advancement, why were so many whites moving into suburban homes, miles from the nearest black family? Since the 1920s, there had been a steady and continuing flight of blacks from the South to the northern cities, where they sought to escape from demeaning segregation, low pay, and poor working conditions. Whites in the South had lived among blacks for years. But many white people in the North had never known African-Americans well and feared staying in the city neighborhoods into which black families from the South had moved. They were afraid of possible violence, and believed that black neighbors would lower the value of their homes. As whites left the inner cities, new suburbs sprawled across the United States. Multilane highways were built to speed middle-class white people safely into and out of cities that became increasingly African-American, Hispanic, or poor — or a combination of all of these. By the end of the 1950s, one-third of all Americans lived in the suburbs.

Americans also began to head for the sunshine and towards the land of opportunity. During each year of the 1950s, nearly one-fifth of the population changed homes. Many headed for the West and the Southwest. Populations in Phoenix, Albuquerque, Houston, and Dallas soared, while California, the most popular resting place, had surpassed New York as the nation's most populous state by 1963.

News reached the suburbs, cities, and villages more and more by television. In 1947, there were only ten thousand TV sets in the United States. By 1957, television was in forty million homes. TV baby-sat children and entertained and informed everyone else. Where families once had gathered around the radio for news, music, and drama, they now sat in living rooms illuminated each evening by the milky grey light of the twelve-inch Crosley or the sixteen-inch Philco televisions. Jokes, opinions, and news films were seen and immediately shared by millions.

When Newton N. Minow, chairman of the Federal Communications Commission, called television "a vast wasteland," many Americans agreed with him. But TV did, nevertheless, play a vital role in informing the American public, verbally and visually, on news and current affairs.

Suffering Heroes

To many of the nation's youth, the feeling about life at the time was one of alienation — of individuals as outsiders. What could cause such a feeling?

This alienation was expressed first in foreign art and literature. Unconventional plays such as Samuel Beckett's *Waiting for Godot*, in 1952, or novels such as Alain Robbe-Grillet's *Voyeur,* in 1955, were widely staged or read. The theme was picked up in the United States by Jack Kerouac, whose 1957 novel, *On the Road*, became the Bible for the nonconformists known as the Beat generation. Many of these Beatniks, who rejected the values of most Americans, agreed with the theme of David Riesman's book, *The Lonely Crowd*. Riesman said that Americans were no longer individuals but instead sought approval of others before taking any kind of action.

Hollywood portrayed alienation in movies such as *On the Waterfront*, starring Marlon Brando, in 1954, and *Rebel Without a Cause*, with James Dean, in 1955. Both actors played loners who suffered because they were unlike everybody else. Dean's death in 1955 immortalized him, even though he had made only three movies before slamming his Porsche

Actor James Dean came to personify alienated youth for generations to come, thanks to his untimely death in an automobile accident and his starring role as a restless teenager in Rebel Without a Cause, *in 1955.*

into a telephone pole on a lonely California highway. Dean and singer Elvis Presley became models for teenage boys who either felt they were — or who wanted to be — on the outside looking in.

Art and Literature

New York City was the world capital of serious painting. The critics loved abstract art, even if the public did not. Many ordinary viewers thought that the lack of any recognizable object in an abstract painting made it silly or worthless. Abstract art continued to increase in value into the 1960s, although it failed to grab public attention in the way that pop art would later in the decade.

Several world-renowned literary careers were winding down — Ernest Hemingway won a Pulitzer Prize for *The Old Man and the Sea* in 1953, and William Faulkner won in 1955 for *A Fable*. These particular prizes were awarded on the basis of the long and distinguished careers of these writers, not the individual work itself. The most talented American composers included Gian Carlo Menotti and Samuel Barber, while Tennessee Williams and Eugene O'Neill, not yet in the twilight of their careers, won Pulitzer Prizes for their dramas.

> *"If I could just do it over, I would do it better, maybe even right."*
>
> William Faulkner, 1950

A Woman's Place

From the comfort of their homes in the suburbs, some white, middle-class women began to question their traditional roles in the family and the wider society. However, traditional female stereotypes still prevailed. Role models such as diver Patty McCormick, winner of gold medals at the 1952 and 1956 Olympics, were less important than film actresses. June Allison, Doris Day, or Grace Kelly might be courageous, funny, or calm and collected, but they also were dependent on leading men in their films. How long would U.S. women accept second-class status? Were women born only to have babies and keep house? If a career was supposed to be an ultimate goal, what of women who *wanted* to be just wives or mothers?

Science came to the rescue of many women with the birth control pill. Available by prescription, the Pill meant that women could decide whether to become pregnant and how many children to have. First used in 1954, the Pill became widely used in the 1960s and helped end the baby boom. It also allowed married women to join or rejoin the work force without fear of pregnancy.

So, an increasing number of mothers headed off to work each morning, even though their pay was only a fraction of their husbands'. Two incomes bought the newly popular huge, heavy cars with chrome bumpers, wide, white-sidewall tires, and pointed fins. The added income also was spent on TV dinners, TV trays (spindly tables that let families dine in front of the television), metal-framed furniture, and refrigerators and stoves in colors such as lagoon blue and buttercup yellow. Electrical appliances became available as smaller push-button models.

With modern conveniences and with the forty-hour work week, there was concern about the effects of too much leisure time. Gardening, yard work, and televised sports failed to keep everyone out of trouble.

The sixties saw a huge increase in demand for convenience foods. TV was beginning to have a growing impact, not just on Americans' leisure time, but on their eating habits, too. This 1961 ad was for one of the earliest brands of TV dinners.

The 1950s drug of choice among adults was alcohol. Skillful beer, wine, and liquor advertising showed handsome, wealthy, well-dressed people relaxing over drinks. The ads did not show the violence, neglect, abuse, and illness also associated with excessive drinking, most of which took place in the home. Domestic discord was on the rise. Divorces totalled nearly 400,000 during each year of the fifties, almost one-quarter the number of marriages.

Outside the home, churches and public buildings took on strange appearances, probably because the shapes most copied by architects were boomerangs, atoms, and flying saucers. New homes were inviting; they were carefully landscaped and filled with furniture. But new buildings looked like glass and steel cages. A troubled churchgoer might find his or her garage or screened-in porch more comforting than the nearby house of worship. Public housing looked more normal, perhaps because it was conceived by the government and constructed by the lowest bidder. Sadly, many high-rise public housing developments would later become no better than vertical slums.

Urban Blight

Age and neglect also caught up with many older downtown areas.

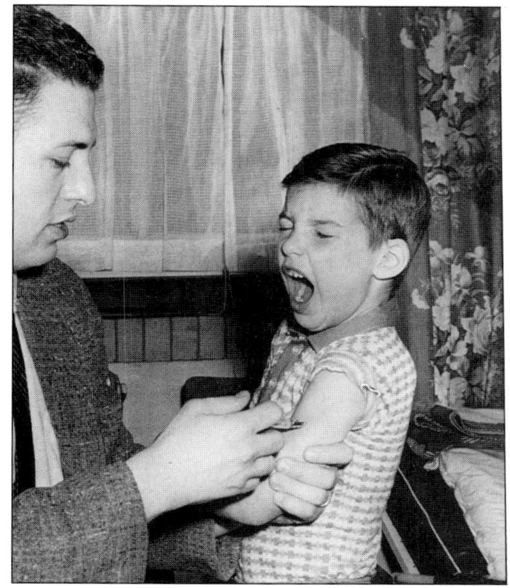

Vaccinations were a new — and obviously mixed — experience for these two young boys in 1961, taking part in tests for a new measles vaccine in Buffalo, New York.

Pittsburgh sometimes turned on its streetlights at noon to cut through smoke and soot from nearby steel mills. Executives went out wearing white shirts and watched them turn gray over lunch hour. In Los Angeles, which had scrapped public transportation for freeways, car exhaust made the air thick with smog. In small towns with a single huge and smoky industry, people died young from lung cancer and other breathing disorders. Was there a connection between dirty air and early death? Would the country develop a national program to clear the air and clean lakes and streams? Or would citizens continue to breathe bad air as the price of progress?

Reform-minded people looked increasingly to Washington for answers. They did so because state and local governments often were run by dishonest hacks. Building inspectors, aldermen, even the police could look the other way when they witnessed corrupt practices and some took money to do so. Corruption was common in labor unions, too. Organized crime frequently ran union locals, taking payoffs from businesses to keep radical union organizers away. Hypocrisy — saying one thing and doing another — seemed common among 1950s adults. So did greed, prejudice, and jealousy. Baby boomers, some of whom had reached high school by 1960, wondered if they would have to lie or cheat or steal in order to survive as young adults.

These young people in particular benefited from medical progress during the Eisenhower era. Penicillin had proven its infection-fighting ability in World War II, and it saved thousands who might otherwise have died from influenza, pneumonia, and related diseases. Other antibiotics worked equally well. The polio vaccine and oral polio doses curbed this widespread crippler of children, while a vaccine for measles was also perfected. Childhood illnesses such as mumps, measles, and whooping cough struck fewer American boys and girls as

(Opposite) Lever House, Park Avenue and 51st Street, New York City, erected in 1952, was typical of the new style of office buildings that were to change city skylines across the world during the fifties and sixties. These huge structures were often built from steel and glass, favoring a clean, simple, angular look. Architects of the time shunned any extraneous or non-functional decorative features.

preventive shots became widespread.

Calling the 1950s "The American Decade" is probably accurate. While most of the rest of the world was still reeling from the effects of World War II, U.S. goods were in demand worldwide, U.S. troops were mobile enough to become engaged around the world, from Korea to Lebanon, and U.S. transportation, communications, and medicine were the envy of the rest of the world. Despite advances in racial integration, space exploration, and agriculture, no one knew what to call the 1960s. By the time the decade ended, the United States was a very different place, forged by earth-shattering events no one could have predicted.

Ten Troubled Years

The war in Vietnam became a funnel into which young American lives were poured. The primitive and simple North Vietnamese and Viet Cong guerrillas, fighting on their own ground, were teaching U.S. soldiers and politicians that weapons and technology could be overcome by skill, courage, and a willingness to die. Americans were increasingly against sending sons, brothers, and husbands into battle on the underbelly of Asia, half a world away. U.S. deaths in Vietnam at the end of 1969 totaled forty thousand, despite the fact that the number of U.S. forces was slowly being reduced in the poor, muggy, and war-torn country.

VIETNAM WAR

For further information see primary source entries on pages

12: 1638-43, 1660-63

Death made headlines at home, too. President John F. Kennedy was killed by one or more rifle bullets while riding in an open car on a visit to Dallas in 1963. Adding to the tragedy, Kennedy's brother, Robert, was shot to death in Los Angeles in 1968 while seeking the presidency. Martin Luther King, Jr., the African-American civil rights leader, also died in 1968. He was similarly gunned down in Memphis.

Death occurred in other ways as illegal drug use became widespread. Amphetamines, heroin, LSD, marijuana — these and other drugs were used by teenagers and young adults. Drugs were used in the military, in college football locker rooms, in school halls, and in the streets. By the decade's end, drug deaths among rock stars had become regular occurrences.

Drug use was also a reaction to the middle-class lifestyle. Millions of young people decided they did not want to become like their parents and attempted to create an alternative to established middle-class life, called the counterculture. With long hair, colorful and funky clothing, psychedelic art, communal living, attempts to practice and spread the idea of world peace — all to the background beat of rock 'n' roll — these wealthy white children from the suburbs became known as flower children or hippies.

The counterculture was made up of numerous groups with different goals. What united them all was the rejection of prevailing middle-class values and the stifling atmosphere of suburban conformity.

Radical politics, fanned by flames of an ongoing war, tried but failed to win over the hippies. Most shrugged at the idea of political activity and turned up the volume on their reel-to-reel tape recorders and stereo record players. Or they were social or weekend hippies, changing clothes and showing up fresh and clean at an office on Monday mornings. Many members of the New Left, as young radicals were called, were intelligent, intense, and often angry. Their homes were the college campuses, student apartments, and urban areas where they met, planned, sat in, fought, and eventually split over issues such as the use of violence to achieve their ends.

Hippies and radicals frequently got along well with African-Americans. Many whites had been radicalized after joining the civil rights movement. For them, Black Power demands were not just reasonable, they were long overdue.

Blacks, meanwhile, so long oppressed and unjustly treated by the white majority, had had enough. Radical blacks, and some whites alike, became more extreme, openly advocating the killing of police out of self defense in some cases. Their attempts at nonviolent protest and integration had been met by violence and hatred. By the end of the decade, police, firefighters, and even the military had firsthand exposure to radical Black Power violence as Los Angeles, Detroit, and other inner cities with African-American populations were set afire.

Other minorities gained attention in other ways. Mexican-American farm workers didn't riot. Instead, they began calling themselves Chicanos, formed the United Farmworkers Union, and boycotted produce such as grapes to protest low pay and bad working conditions of migrant farm workers. American Indians, many of whom lived on reservations, were slower to organize. But by the end of the decade, some tribes were insisting that the federal government honor treaties that would give land back to the country's first inhabitants. Other minorities thrived: Japanese-Americans, for example, went about their business, becoming wealthier and better educated than any other minority — or the majority, for that matter.

This left what Richard Nixon in 1969 would label the "silent majority" to fight the wars, put out the fires, rebuild the cities, pay the taxes, and run the country. Radicals tried but failed to win over working people. Instead, many blue-collar workers became more conservative or forgot about politics altogether as their hopes and dreams burned in rioting or died in a jungle or were belittled by better-educated sons and daughters of the middle class. In less than a decade, the country went from a more or less united people to dozens of groups who considered outsiders enemies. How could it have happened?

U.S. athletes Tom Smith and John Carlos made sports history in the 1968 Olympics at Mexico City, where they had taken first and third place in the 200 meter dash. They displayed the "Black Power" gesture of bowed head and clenched fist in a black glove during the playing of the national anthem at the awards ceremony after the race.

CHAPTER 2
John F. Kennedy and Camelot

The Kennedys pose as a family group at the start of a new decade. President-elect John F. Kennedy is flanked by his parents and his wife Jacqueline, together with his brothers and sisters and their respective wives and husbands. Some of the family members would have an influential hand in the Kennedy administration of the next few years. As a family, they were destined to play a memorable part in this era of American history.

Even though he was elected America's thirty-fifth president by only one hundred thousand votes, John F. Kennedy enjoyed wide popularity. A war hero, a U.S. Senator, a Democrat, and a Roman Catholic, Kennedy was a member of a wealthy, large, and powerful Massachusetts family. A youthful forty-three when elected president, JFK proved it by playing informal touch football games. The public and the media enjoyed his ability to handle tough questions with a sharp wit and an ever-ready smile.

In a stirring acceptance speech following his 1960 presidential nomination, Kennedy had spelled out his vision for the nation: "We stand today on the edge of a new frontier — the frontier of the 1960s, a frontier of unknown opportunities and paths, a frontier of unfulfilled hopes and threats."

Kennedy's "New Frontier" was less an organized set of legislative initiatives, like the New Deal of the thirties, or Johnson's "Great Society" yet to come. It was more a personal vision of the young president — an ideology that was progressive, but by no means radical.

Kennedy versus Nixon

Kennedy's foe in the 1960 election was Richard M. Nixon. A California Republican, Nixon was a logical candidate; he had served eight years as vice president under Dwight Eisenhower. Both Kennedy and Nixon were well known as anticommunists, with Kennedy a liberal and Nixon a conservative. Both were considered moderate in terms of social policy. They squared off in a series of television debates that showed both men to have an excellent grasp of issues facing the country. Unfortunately for Nixon, he looked older, tired, and in need of a shave. Those who listened to the debates on the radio called the contests even, but TV viewers gave Kennedy a distinct edge, with his youthful looks, relaxed manner, and perhaps more presidential bearing.

Republicans still claim that the 1960 presidential election was stolen by the mayor of Chicago at the time, Richard J. Daley. That may be true — Daley headed a Democratic political machine that reminded people to "vote early and often." Chicago's avalanche of votes gave Kennedy the state of Illinois and just enough electoral college votes to win. Feelings really did run high. A farm boy from a Protestant, Republican family living in Indiana said the day after the election, "My grandmother read the newspaper, spit on the front page, and had a stroke!"

The new president soon appointed a host of young, liberal minded anticommunists and professors or graduates of Harvard and other Ivy League colleges. Robert McNamara, formerly president of the Ford Motor Company, became secretary of defense; an academic, McGeorge Bundy, was special assistant for national security; while the president's younger brother, Bobby Kennedy, was appointed attorney general. The average age of Kennedy's cabinet was forty-seven, ten years younger than Eisenhower's. Kennedy's aim was clearly to give the impression of a president and cabinet full of the energy and drive needed to meet the challenges of the New Frontier. Kennedy rejected the staff system. As one political commentator wrote, "Eisenhower wanted decisions brought to him for approval [but] Kennedy wanted problems brought to him for decision."

Kennedy's team were widely pictured to live in "Camelot," that is, the legendary place where King Arthur held court, and also the title of a popular Broadway play running at that time. A book about them called the advisors *The Best and the Brightest.* What is perhaps most unique about them to people now is that they believed they could solve any and all of the country's problems as well as those around the world through technology and social engineering.

Kennedy was a published author and a hero in the U.S. Navy in World War II. When aboard a torpedo boat in the Pacific, he was seriously injured in a clash with a Japanese destroyer. He suffered through three operations on his back and was in pain much of

"And so, my fellow Americans: ask not what your country can do for you — ask what you can do for your country."

President John F. Kennedy during his inaugural address in Washington, D.C., in 1961

"A man does what he must — in spite of personal consequences, in spite of obstacles and dangers — and that is the basis of all human morality."

John F. Kennedy, *Profiles in Courage,* 1955

On one of his weekly television appearances from Havana, Fidel Castro claimed that a U.S. reconnaissance plane had been sighted photographing a Soviet merchant ship only ten miles from the coast of Cuba. The U.S. had already broken off diplomatic relations with Cuba before Kennedy became president, when Castro seized power in Cuba in 1959, nationalized all American businesses, and signed a trade agreement with Moscow. In 1961, John F. Kennedy referred to Cuba as: "a Communist satellite on our very doorstep."

his adult life. Nevertheless, he served from 1947 to 1953 in the House of Representatives and in the Senate from 1953 to 1960.

Kennedy proved to be a strong candidate, surprising the experts by winning the Democratic Party primary in overwhelmingly religious, Protestant West Virginia. The Catholic senator believed in the separation of church and state, in labor reform, and in aid to emerging nations in Latin America, Asia, and Africa. He was handsome and had an attractive wife and small children.

All of this added up to a very narrow victory over Nixon, who won his own home state of California, but lost several other very close state contests to fall only 118,550 votes short from a total of 68.3 million votes cast. Nixon might also have won had he not been blamed for the nation's sluggish economy under President Eisenhower. Nixon lost the governor's race in California two years later, and bitterly promised the news media that "You won't have Richard Nixon to kick around any more." It proved to be a promise the lawyer, politician, and future president would not keep.

The entire Kennedy family proved popular, especially with African-Americans, but also with other ethnic groups, and with the nation's poor. As attorney general, Bobby Kennedy ran a Justice Department that became increasingly sensitive to minority issues. Edward, the president's youngest brother, was elected in 1962 to John's former Senate seat in Massachusetts. A young mother, Jacqueline Bouvier Kennedy had a great deal of experience in Washington, having lived and worked there as a news photographer. Unlike most first ladies, she knew how the system worked. Sargent Shriver, the husband of the president's sister, became director of the Peace Corps. Another brother-in-law, Stephen Smith, would prepare to run the 1964 presidential campaign.

The Bay of Pigs

Early in his first term, Kennedy faced a crisis in foreign affairs. In 1959, the Central Intelligence Agency (CIA) was beginning to train anti-communist Cuban exiles for an invasion of their homeland. Fidel Castro, who had led a revolution in Cuba in the 1950s, had emerged as a Communist dictator by 1960. The U.S. military told Kennedy that the minute the anti-Castro Cubans landed, an anti-Castro uprising would occur. But the invasion fell apart; every man who hit the beach at the Bay of Pigs was either killed or captured. Kennedy accepted responsibility for the fiasco in public, but blamed U.S. generals in private for bad advice. A political cartoon at the time showed Kennedy talking into a telephone: "That's the last time I let Caroline [his infant daughter] plan an invasion!"

Due in part to the calamity in Cuba, Soviet Premier Nikita Khrushchev believed he could get the better of Kennedy in showdowns between communism and democracy. For example, in 1961, Khrushchev ordered a wall built between East and West Berlin. Kennedy quickly sent U.S. National Guard and reserve troops to Germany, and Khrushchev backed down. A year later, he was busy sending Soviet technicians and missiles with nuclear warheads to Fidel Castro. Again, Kennedy held firm, forcing the Communists to remove the warheads, and the two nuclear superpowers retreated after pushing each other toward the brink of nuclear war.

Waiting for Their Rights

One remarkable feature of the federal government at the time was its lack of a serious response to appeals by African-Americans for enforcement of school integration, voting, and other laws. African-Americans, who had so long waited for the federal government to help them gain equal treatment, eventually got tired of waiting. During Dwight Eisenhower's final year as president, four black college students sat down at a segregated Woolworth's lunch counter in Greensboro, North Carolina, and refused to move after being denied service. Other variety stores and lunch counters were the sites of similar confrontations. By the eighth month of the Kennedy administration in September 1961, some seventy thousand black and white Americans joined the protest.

Meanwhile, during the spring of 1961, busloads of "freedom riders," organized by the Congress of Racial Equality (CORE) and the Student Nonviolent Coordinating Committee (SNCC) were leaving Washington, D.C., bound for the South. There, the black and white riders hoped to monitor southern compliance with recently enacted federal regulations for desegregation.

This twenty-one-year-old student was a casualty of the 1961 Freedom Ride Campaign organized by the Congress of Racial Equality and members of the Student Nonviolent Coordinating Committee. A series of racially integrated bus rides were intended to tour the South and test the region's compliance with the newly enacted desegregation orders. Freedom riders were harassed and attacked along the route, and there was such a bad outbreak of mob violence in Montgomery that a bus was fire bombed. The Kennedy administration was forced to restore order by sending in federal marshals.

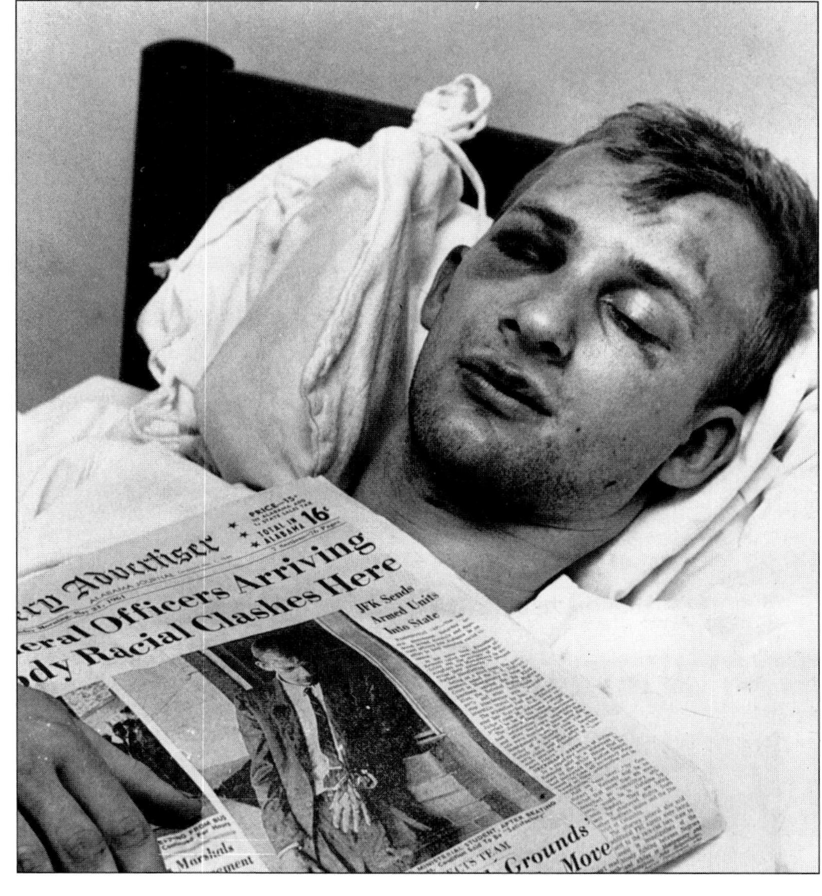

(Opposite) Martin Luther King, Jr. waving to participants of the 1963 Civil Rights March on Washington. It was here he made his moving and world-famous speech beginning: "I have a dream that one day this nation will rise up and live out the true meaning of its creed."

Martin Luther King, Jr. (1929-1968)

The son of a minister, King was born in Atlanta and showed very early that he was an unusually intelligent student. By the age of fifteen, he was in college, studying sociology. A college graduate at nineteen, he attended a seminary in Pennsylvania and went on to earn a doctorate in theology at Boston University. By the time he was twenty-five, he was married and had assumed full responsibility for the Dexter Avenue Church in Montgomery, Alabama.

A year later, a black woman by the name of Rosa Parks defied a Montgomery ordinance that segregated seating on buses. This propelled King, along with Edward Nixon and Reverend Ralph Abernathy, into leading the successful Montgomery bus boycott. He then traveled, meditated, wrote, and delivered speeches. Visiting Africa and India, King was impressed with the emergence of new nations and with the idea of winning political and racial disputes through nonviolent protest.

On September 20, 1958, while autographing the book he wrote about the bus boycott, *Stride Toward Freedom*, King was stabbed by a deranged black woman. He survived and was asked to assume a bigger role in the civil rights struggle. King accepted the presidency of the Southern Christian Leadership Conference and moved to SCLC headquarters in Atlanta in 1960. He lent moral and financial support to another Atlanta-based organization, the Student Nonviolent Coordinating Committee. King's organization and SNCC (usually pronounced "Snick") would be at the helm of civil rights in the South.

Martin Luther King, Jr. leads the Selma-to-Montgomery civil rights march in Alabama, 1965.

Taking on the white power structure had its price. King was jailed and even put into prison without any kind of hearing in Georgia following a sit-in at a department store lunch counter. Besides encouraging southern blacks to register as voters, he played major roles in desegregation activities in Albany, Georgia, and Montgomery, Alabama. His "I have a dream" speech electrified the March on Washington in 1963 and he was *Time* magazine's "Man of the Year" in 1964 — the first black person so honored.

King led marchers from Selma, Alabama, to Montgomery in a march that showed black militants to be impatient with nonviolence since his marches and demonstrations frequently ended in mass arrests that showed no immediate results. The minister also had mixed success in civil rights work in Chicago and in Mississippi, again bumping into impatient militants such as Stokely Carmichael and his Black Power followers. In April, 1967, he joined singer Harry Belafonte, pediatrician Dr. Benjamin Spock, and others in denouncing U.S. participation in the Vietnam War.

King realized that he was seen as a racial moderate by many of his people. He pondered his role and that of the black citizen in American society, concluding that "a revolution of values" had to take place for African-Americans to be treated equally. He hoped that his long-time allies — labor unions, liberals, students, intellectuals, and the churches — would pressure the government for reform.

King was shot to death on April 4, 1968, while on a trip to Memphis, Tennessee, to show support for the city's mostly black garbage collectors, who had been on strike for several months. He left behind his father, mother, widow, and four children. President Jimmy Carter, also a Georgia native, posthumously awarded him the Medal of Freedom, the nation's highest civilian honor, in 1977.

"I have a dream that one day on the red hills of Georgia the sons of former slaves and the sons of former slave-owners will be able to sit down together at the table of brotherhood.

I have a dream that one day even the state of Mississippi, a state sweltering with the people's injustice, sweltering with the heat of oppression, will be transformed into an oasis of freedom and justice.

I have a dream that my four little children will one day live in a nation where they will not be judged by the color of their skin but by the content of their character."

Martin Luther King, 1963 March on Washington

The freedom riders were greeted on their arrival by mobs of southern whites, who attacked, harassed, and viciously beat the demonstrators. Following a particularly violent attack in Montgomery, Alabama, Attorney General Robert Kennedy was prompted to send out six hundred federal marshals to restore order. Martial law was declared in Alabama and twenty-seven of the riders were arrested in Jackson, Mississippi.

On August 28, 1963, civil rights workers decided to stage a "March on Washington for Jobs and Freedom." The march was to show support for a civil rights bill before Congress. But it also became a forum for blacks and whites to tell the nation about racial injustice in the South. Because it was the first big Washington rally since before World War II, the march was nationally televised. It showed a mixed crowd of 200,000 persons listening peacefully to white performers like Bob Dylan and to black leaders like Martin Luther King, Jr. There, in front of the Lincoln Monument, Dr. King gave his most famous speech, which included the refrain, "I have a

> *"How many men must die before we can really have a free and true and peaceful society? How long will it take?"*
>
> Coretta Scott King

dream," and which conveyed the minister's fervent hopes for an integrated, fair United States.

Seeds of Change

Had white American males — the people in power when the sixties began — noticed, they would have detected a rage all through twentieth-century African-American literature. Writers such as Langston Hughes in the 1930s, Richard Wright in the 1940s, and James Baldwin in the 1950s foresaw trouble brewing from America's unequal treatment of its black citizens. It is to the credit of African-Americans — and to a few progressives — that they tried to obtain equality peacefully before going after it with fire and weapons.

An unlikely pacifist heroine had emerged several years earlier, in 1955, and her actions would help form the shape and use of civil disobedience in the sixties' civil rights movement. Her name was Rosa Parks, and she made headlines because her feet hurt. "I had been working all day, handling clothes that white people wear" in a dry-cleaning store, she explained. When the middle-aged resident of Montgomery, Alabama, climbed on her bus and sank into a seat, she was in no mood to obey the driver, who yelled "Niggers move back" to make room for white riders. Mrs. Parks refused to move. Her arrest and the resulting boycott of Montgomery buses by African-Americans was a benchmark in the peaceful move toward equality on public transportation in the segregated South. Rosa Parks symbolized passive resistance, taught by Martin Luther King, Jr., and practiced repeatedly wherever there was discrimination. But King was not the only African-American leader formed in the fifties and leading through the sixties.

A. Philip Randolph was also typical of the kind of person who shaped the civil rights movement. Born in Florida in 1889, he moved to Harlem in 1911 and attended college by night. By day, he and others tried to organize black workers so they could enjoy benefits similar to those being won by white union members. Randolph became a railroad porter and quickly organized fellow black porters. In 1939, he and his members won their first major contract. As World War II began, he persuaded President Franklin D. Roosevelt to put an end to discrimination in the defense industries.

After World War II, Randolph's campaigning resulted in an order by President Harry Truman to desegregate the armed forces. When the American Federation of Labor merged with the Congress of Industrial Organizations in 1955, Randolph was named a vice president. This tall, thin son of a Methodist minister also helped organize the 1963 March on Washington and founded an institute for the study of chronic poverty.

Among civil rights challenges was the resurgence of the Ku Klux Klan. Formed after the Civil War as an underground, southern terrorist organization, the Klan had declined in popularity after the 1920s, but resurfaced to oppose the civil rights movement. Several hundred "redneck" (rural or working-class) white Christian males made up its membership. They attempted, with bullets and bombs, to stop legislation giving African-Americans voting and other rights.

Civil Rights

For further information see primary source entries on pages

11: 1582-83; **12:** 1627-32, 1635-38, 1643-50, 1652-55

Some 1,000 men, women, and children gathered to hear Imperial Wizard Robert Shelton speak from the rostrum at an open-field Ku Klux Klan rally in North Carolina in 1965. During his speech, Shelton denied accusations by President Johnson that the KKK was responsible for violence in Alabama.

Though small in number (there were only around 10,000 committed dues-paying KKK members and around 100,000 hangers-on during the sixties), the group was of enough importance that in 1965, President Lyndon Johnson denounced it on national television.

Supreme Court Cases

African-Americans continued to claim their rights, even if it took troops to do so. In Oxford, Mississippi, in the fall of 1962, three thousand federal troops were sent to the University of Mississippi so that James Meredith could be the first black student to enroll there. His courageous move could be traced back to 1954, the year the Supreme Court ruled, in *Brown v. Board of Education,* that separate schools for black and white students were inherently unequal. The Brown decision made state-approved segregation in public schools illegal because it was seen to violate the equal protection clause of the Fourteenth Amendment to the Constitution. During both the Kennedy and Johnson administrations, several other far-reaching rulings would be handed down by an increasingly liberal Supreme Court:

- *Mapp v. Ohio*, 1961. The Court ruled that police could not use evidence in a state or federal trial that was seized without a reasonable suspicion to search for it in the first place. What the Court believed, but did not say outright, was that defendants deserved fairer treatment by law enforcement than they had been getting up to now.
- *Engel v. Vitale*, 1962. Public school officials could not require pupils to recite a state-composed prayer at the start of each school day, even if the prayer was not associated with a particular religion and pupils could be excused from reciting it.

RACE

For further information see primary source entries on pages

11: 1460-64, 1474-75, 1504-05, 1518-19

The justices felt that such state approval of religious speeches was an unconstitutional attempt to establish religion. This would be contrary to the First Amendment provision that "Congress shall make no law respecting the establishment of religion."

- *Gideon v. Wainwright*, 1963. The Court ruled that the due process clause of the Fourteenth Amendment extended to state as well as federal defendants. This meant that all persons charged with serious crimes must be provided with an attorney, and states were required to appoint attorneys for defendants unable to pay their own legal fees.
- *New York Times Co. v. Sullivan*, 1964. The Supreme Court ruled here that the First Amendment guarantee of freedom of the press protected the press from libel suits for reports that damaged the reputation of public officials unless the officials proved that the reports resulted from actual malicious intent.
- *Griswold v. Connecticut*, 1965. The Court ruled that a state illegally interfered with personal privacy in the marriage relationship when it prohibited anyone, including all married couples, from using contraceptives.
- *Miranda v. Arizona*, 1966. The Court decided that the guarantee of due process required that, before any questioning of suspects in police cus-

Thurgood Marshall. (1908-1993)

Thurgood Marshall, retired U.S. Supreme Court justice and a black man, is as responsible as anyone for the strides made by African-Americans in this century.

Marshall was born and reared in Baltimore, a city with northern industries and southern sympathies. He graduated from Lincoln University in 1930 and held other real and honorary degrees, including a law degree. He was honored by universities from Liberia to New Zealand.

The bespectacled attorney gained his experience by serving almost fifteen years as special counsel to the National Association for the Advancement of Colored People (the NAACP). He also directed the NAACP's legal defense and education fund.

As word of his ability spread, he was nominated in 1961 to the U.S. Circuit Court, a federal position. Lyndon Johnson named him solicitor general, second only to the attorney general in power, in 1965. Two years later, the president selected him for the U.S. Supreme Court. From 1967 to 1991, he consistently voted for the liberal side of cases before him and his fellow justices.

Marshall successfully argued *Brown v. the Board of Education of Topeka, Kansas*, the landmark civil rights decision in 1954. After hearing Marshall's thoughts, the Supreme Court ruled that keeping blacks and whites in separate school systems was unconstitutional, even when blacks were given equal facilities. Marshall is known for other courageous work, including traveling to Korea to ensure that black soldiers were given equal treatment in military trials.

He retired in 1991, but not before criticizing the Supreme Court nominees of Ronald Reagan and George Bush. He felt their choices were too oriented toward the nominees' beliefs on single issues and were too conservative. At his death in January, 1993, presidents, statesmen, ordinary men and women, both black and white, and hundreds of children filed by his casket to mourn the outspoken jurist.

tody, the suspects must be informed of their right to remain silent, that anything they say may be used against them, and their right to counsel.

Clearly, the U.S. Supreme Court under Chief Justice Earl Warren, an Eisenhower appointee, thought the earlier scales had been tipped too far in favor of government and law enforcement. Why else insist that a person suspected of a crime be told about options in the familiar words that began, "You have the right to remain silent. . . ."? The Court soon became a politically charged issue, especially for Nixon and other conservatives, like right-wing Arizona Republican Barry Goldwater.

A Crime in the Making: the Assassination

In November, 1963, President Kennedy decided to tour the western United States to strengthen his political standing there. He suspected his Republican opponent in the 1964 presidential election would be Barry Goldwater, and he wanted to be seen in a part of the country that would most strongly back the senator from Arizona. The president also wanted to stop in Texas, where a rift in the Democratic Party was making Republicans stronger by the day. On Friday, November 22, 1963, he and

President and Mrs. Kennedy settle themselves in the rear seats of their automobile at the start of a motorcade into the city of Dallas, November 22, 1963. Since the weather that day was so lovely, the president asked that the car's protective bubble be removed. He was soon to be gunned down by a sniper as the vehicle travelled through the downtown area.

Within hours of Kennedy's assassination, Lee Harvey Oswald was arrested and charged with his murder. Two days later, Oswald himself was shot dead by Jack Ruby, a Dallas nightclub owner, as he was being transferred to a tighter security prison.

Mrs. Kennedy were riding slowly in a Lincoln convertible through downtown Dallas when there was gunfire at about 12:30 P.M.

Two bullets struck the president. He was pronounced dead at nearby Parkland Memorial Hospital about an hour later. Texas Governor John Connally was also hit and gravely wounded but he recovered. Lyndon Johnson took the oath of office as president at 2:38 P.M. Lee Harvey Oswald, a resident of Dallas and only twenty-four years old, was accused of killing the president. Two days later, on live, national television, Oswald was shot and killed by Jack Ruby, a local nightclub owner, in the basement of the Dallas police station.

But Who Was Behind the Killing?

Those are the bare facts. But the more the public learned, the more confused everyone became. If only two bullets were fired, who, then, shot Governor Connally? Could any marksman shoot a moving target one hundred and eighty feet away in under three seconds, with a gun that was notorious for its inability to hit a target? Was John F. Kennedy lured to Dallas so he could be killed? Were Cuban Communists, angry at America's attempted assassination of Fidel Castro, behind the slaying? Or were anti-Castro Cubans possibly involved as a result of Kennedy's refusal to invade Cuba? Oswald had spent some time in the Soviet Union and was known to have Cuban sympathies. Was he part of a wider conspiracy?

Vice President Lyndon B. Johnson was sworn in aboard the presidential plane before it returned to Washington. On his right is his wife, Ladybird, and on his left, Jacqueline Kennedy, the widow of the assassinated president.

Could the killing have been a coup — a planned event so that Lyndon Johnson could take over the government? Or were sinister forces within the FBI or the CIA involved in some kind of complex assassination plot?

President Johnson, sensitive to possible criticism, appointed a panel of famous citizens to look into Kennedy's assassination. The Warren Commission, as it came to be known, spent nearly a year interviewing people and compiling information. On September 27, 1964, the commission issued a report stating that President Kennedy was killed by a lone gunman, Lee Harvey Oswald. Even though the commission released twenty-six volumes of testimony and evidence, not everyone agreed with the conclusion. Within a few years, so many controversies about the assassination had developed that *Esquire* magazine ran a guide to different theories about who was involved.

The Kennedy assassination and the events surrounding it are something many Americans never forgot. People who had previously felt good about government and the United States became negative, believing that the country was eroding. This notion was reinforced by Lyndon Johnson who, although popular at first, was personally and politically ruined by U.S. involvement in the disasterous war in Vietnam.

"His [President Kennedy's] widow compared the Kennedy years in the White House to Camelot, the site of King Arthur's legendary court.... The romantic hero and heroine, the battle between good and evil, a time of great happiness forever lost — all these images were more commonly applied to ballads and myths than to political figures."

From *American Odyssey: The United States in the Twentieth Century,* edited by Gary B. Nash

Kennedy's Achievements

So what did Kennedy achieve during his three short years in office? Certainly his efforts to perk up the economy contributed to an upswing that continued until the early 1970s. He increased spending on defense and poured millions into a space program and other government programs that increased employment. Through the Area Redevelopment Act, he channeled federal funds into the poorer regions of the country. The minimum wage was raised from $1 to $1.25 an hour, and he steered a major tax cut through the House in 1962, although it was not fully approved by the Senate until after Kennedy's death.

He initiated Head Start, a program which helped preschoolers from disadvantaged families, and attempted to pass an education aid bill, but was stymied by a coalition of Republican and southern Democrats who feared that increased federal support for education would reduce state control. At the time of his assassination, he was asking advisors to draw up a plan to tackle poverty in the nation and he promised further action on civil rights.

Meanwhile, Kennedy was active in promoting overseas development. The Peace Corps was set up to aid developing countries. Its objectives, in Kennedy's own words, were "to liberate independent nations from the bonds of hunger, ignorance and poverty." The program trained Americans of all ages to teach skills in agriculture and public health to local people in poor countries across the world.

In retrospect, very few historians doubt that Kennedy would have won reelection or that such programs as the Peace Corps and Head Start were successes. But many of his achievements are balanced by blunders in foreign policy, like the Bay of Pigs fiasco, and by Vietnam, which could have done to his second four years what it did to Lyndon Johnson after the 1964 election.

CHAPTER 3
Lyndon B. Johnson, the Great Society, and Social Justice

John F. Kennedy was nominated for president overwhelmingly on the first ballot cast at the 1960 Democratic convention. The man he defeated was Lyndon B. Johnson. Johnson was a Texan, a former school teacher, a former congressman, and the leader of the Democrats in the U.S. Senate. Kennedy, a liberal Catholic from Massachusetts, needed a moderate, Protestant southerner such as Johnson to balance the ticket. He asked LBJ to be his vice president. Johnson knew the vice presidency had always been an awkward job, but Kennedy treated him respectfully, and he could hardly decline the request.

Americans living more than a few miles from the nation's capital have always been extremely distrustful of politicians. Lyndon Johnson was seen as a wheeler-dealer who would sacrifice any principle to get his bills passed or to take care of his friends. He had been taught how government worked by President Franklin D. Roosevelt in the 1930s. Roosevelt liked Johnson's loyalty and his ability to correctly size up a political situation. As the 1960s began, Johnson was the Senate majority leader and among the last of a generation identified with the New Deal.

After the 1960 election, Johnson found himself an outsider, disliked by Kennedy's advisors, most of whom were East Coast intellectuals. The vice president intensely disliked and was unable to deal with Robert Kennedy, the new attorney general and presidential brother. But he did all that the president asked of him. Packing his own bed, his own shower nozzle, and his favorite whiskey, he visited twenty-six different countries from 1961 through mid-1963. During one brief stopover in Washington, D.C., he confided to a friend, "My future is behind me."

Taking Command

That, of course, changed in November 1963 with Kennedy's assassination. The nation needed someone to lead who was saddened but still strong — that person could only be Lyndon Johnson. At first, he felt that, "I took the oath, but for millions of Americans I was illegitimate." He was a gangling politician, known as an egotistical bully. And he had to overcome rumors that he may somehow have been a conspirator in the shooting in Dallas.

"All I have I would give gladly not to be here today," he said in his first address to Congress. The speech came to be the most important of his life up to that point. Johnson had reassured Americans in the widely televised address that the government would continue to work. Equally important, he promised to put John F. Kennedy's legacy into practice. "I had

POLITICS

For further information see primary source entries on pages

11: 1482-83; **12:** 1603-04, 1620-24, 1632-35, 1682-85, 1688-89, 1692-94, 1700-01, 1706-09, 1727-30

to take the dead president's program and turn it into a martyr's cause," Johnson later said. "That way, Kennedy would live on forever and so would I."

"The Great Society rests on abundance and liberty for all. It demands an end to poverty and racial injustice....[It] is a place where every child can find knowledge to enrich his mind...where the city of man serves not only the needs of the body and the demands for commerce, but the desire for beauty and the hunger for community."

Lyndon B. Johnson in his opening remarks to a speech at the University of Michigan, 1964

Johnson's Great Society

The new president began to see himself as part of the wide sweep of history, telling friends that civil rights legislation would finish what Abraham Lincoln had begun. Johnson's fellow southern Democrats advised him against legislation that would help minorities. Richard Russell, a senator from Georgia, told him that equality was "a perversion of the American way of life. . . . You may do it, but it will cost you [votes in] the South."

Southern senators began a delaying tactic known as a filibuster that lasted eighty-three days. A filibuster is a tactic whereby politicians speak on a bill almost endlessly, sometimes simply reading from books, in order to stop it ever coming up for a vote. In the Senate, a motion to end a debate, and thus thwart a filibuster, had to be carried by a two-thirds majority. Eventually, the Senate minority leader, Everett McKinley Dirksen, a conservative Republican from Illinois, and no friend of civil rights, ended the suspense by lining up the Republican votes behind the president. The Civil Rights Act of 1964 finally passed.

The act banned discrimination in voting, in hiring, and in the use of virtually all public places. In Mississippi and elsewhere, hundreds

In 1964, President Johnson promised a brighter future for the poverty-stricken like these East Kentucky children, photographed on the porch of their home in a depressed mining community. His genuine concern was converted into practical terms through a series of Great Society programs, which actually reduced the percentage of impoverished Americans during the decade.

of trained and committed northern whites joined southern blacks in registering voters, and June, July, and August 1964 came to be known as Freedom Summer. Some southern whites reacted violently; fifteen civil rights workers, black and white, were murdered. As the summer progressed, some blacks felt nonviolence was no longer the answer.

Johnson was probably the most outspoken president in the twentieth century, with the possible exception of Franklin D. Roosevelt, in advocating the abolition of poverty. Yet he also had wide support from business. As well as the Civil Rights Act, he introduced many other programs during the period 1964-66, which together he termed the "Great Society." The major programs were:

The Economic Opportunity Act (1964). This launched the "war on poverty," his battle to improve living conditions for poor Americans. Out of this bill came nationwide federal funding for programs such as Head Start, which continues today to help disadvantaged children prepare for schooling; the Job Corps, which taught basic skills needed for employment; and Volunteers in Service for America (VISTA), which was a kind of Peace Corps for the home front, where volunteer citizens worked in poor neighborhoods.

The Wilderness Preservation Act (1964). This act set aside 9.1 million acres of forest from commercial development.

The Elementary and Secondary Education

After passage of the Voting Rights Act, African-Americans flocked in large numbers to rural polling places like "The Sugar Shack," a small store in Wilcox County, Alabama. Typical of such rural areas of the South, black voters outnumbered whites by almost three to one.

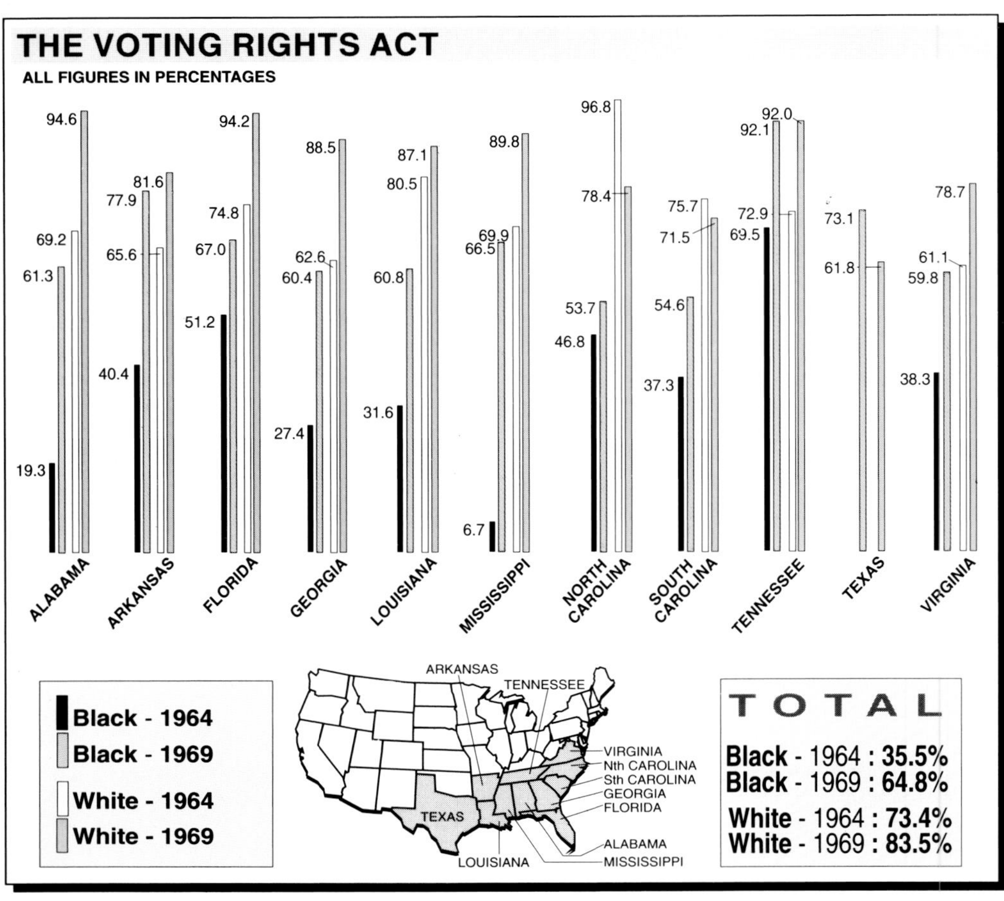

The Voting Rights Act made it illegal to refuse certain minority group voters the right to register, and the percentage of adult white and black registrations in the South changed significantly between 1964 and 1969.

Act (1965). This act introduced the first major federal aid package to education in U.S. history.

The Medical Care Act (1965). This established Medicare, the federally funded program for the elderly, and Medicaid, which provided health care for the younger recipients of welfare. An estimated nineteen million Americans were eligible to receive the new Medicare assistance when it became available.

The Voting Rights Act (1965). This prohibited states from using literacy tests or poll taxes in order to curtail voter registration among minorities and provided for federal supervision of voter registration.

The Omnibus Housing Act (1965). This act provided funds to build and subsidize housing for low-income groups, while the *Model Cities Act (1966)* funded the clearing of slums and created the new department of Housing and Urban Development (HUD), whose secretary, Robert Weaver, became the first African-American cabinet member.

The Water Quality Act (1965). This act required states to analyze and clean up interstate water that flowed within their boundaries.

The National Endowments for the Arts and the Humanities were set up in 1965 to provide aid both to arts organizations and to individual artists.

The Immigration Act (1965). This act all but ended immigrant quotas based on national origin. (Strict immigration quotas had been in force since

1924, when the Immigration Act restricted total annual immigration to 150,000.) The 1965 act raised the annual ceiling to 120,000 western hemisphere immigrants each year and 170,000 from other nations. Johnson hoped to encourage those fleeing oppressive regimes to seek refuge in the U.S. with the words, "The future holds little hope for any government where the present holds no hope for the people."

Two important pieces of consumer legislation were *The Traffic and Motor Vehicle Safety Act (1966)*, which set safety standards in auto and tire manufacturing, and *The Truth in Packaging Act (1966)*, which established standards for the accurate labeling of a whole range of products.

A Landslide Victory

While attempting to set up the first of these programs, Johnson had the 1964 election to win. He and his vice-presidential choice, Senator Hubert Humphrey of Minnesota, were pitted against Republicans Barry Goldwater and William Miller, a congressman from the state of New York. Goldwater came from the right wing of the Republican party, a group known more for boosting the military than for aiding minorities. When Goldwater told voters that "Extremism in the defense of liberty is no vice," many wondered if he might carelessly order military actions that could lead to World War III.

The effects of the Immigration Act of 1965, which ended immigrant quotas based on national origin, can be seen in this map showing the main sources of immigration to the United States in the 1950s and 1970s.

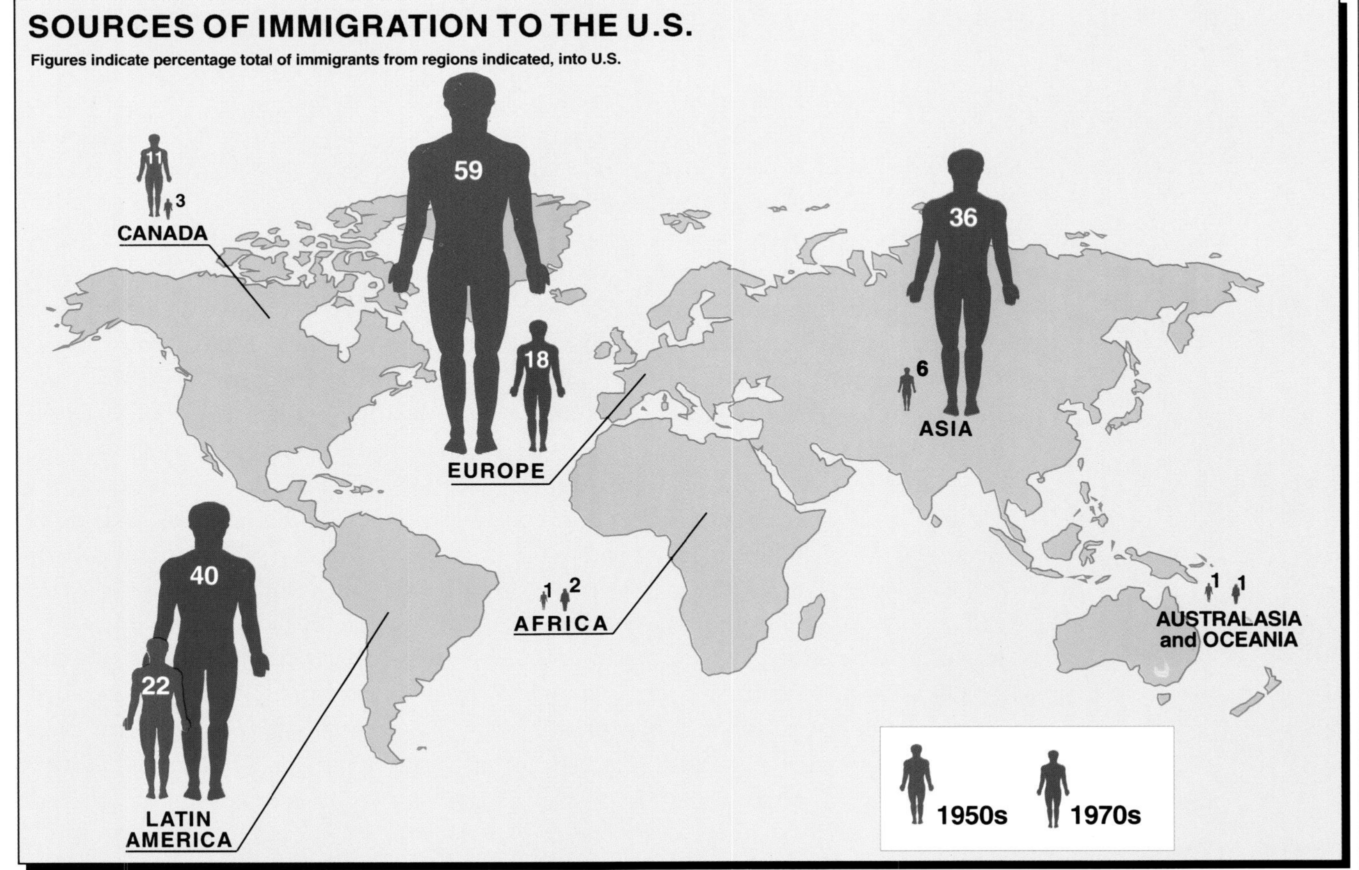

Goldwater's ideology was extreme. He opposed civil rights legislation and progressive federal taxation and wanted to bomb Vietnam. His election propaganda claimed: "In your heart you know he's right." Opponents suggested that, "In your guts, you know he's nuts."

President Johnson did nothing to dispel people's fears of Goldwater's hawkishness. Although his administration secretly had been running operations into North Vietnam for six months, LBJ portrayed himself as the only hope for peace in the 1960s. But perhaps to prove he was no pacifist (called doves at the time), or perhaps to steal the anticommunist high ground from under Goldwater, he publicly ordered troops to punish the North Vietnamese for an alleged attack on a U.S. Navy boat, the *Maddox*, in August, 1964. Johnson pushed through the Tonkin Gulf Resolution by a unanimous vote in the House of Representatives and by an eighty-eight to two margin in the Senate. The resolution handed LBJ a blank check to make war (or to be a hawk, as proponents of war were called) in Vietnam. Looking back on the *Maddox* incident and the lopsided resolution vote, Senator J. William Fulbright of Arkansas said, "I had been taken in."

Johnson then told anyone who would listen that, "I will never send American boys to Vietnam." He won the 1964 election by the largest margin in history. "For the first time in my life, I felt loved by the American people," Johnson said. The love affair would quickly turn sour as the president tried to prop up weak governments in South Vietnam, and to deal with Ho Chi Minh, the elderly leader of the North Vietnamese.

For years, the U.S. had supported the corrupt and undemocratic regime of Ngo Dinh Diem in South Vietnam. In 1954, Eisenhower had put forward the "domino theory" to explain U.S. involvement in Southeast Asia. He believed that if South Vietnam fell to communism, all the other countries in the region would fall in turn like dominoes.

Diem was a brutal dictator. He refused to hold the elections that the Communists would probably have won. An aristocratic Catholic, he ruthlessly persecuted Buddhists, many of whom publicly set fire to themselves in protest. Just before Kennedy's assassination, and with covert U.S. support, the Diem regime was overthrown. By this time there were 16,000 U.S. military advisors in the country. With Kennedy's death, the problem of what to do with South Vietnam fell to Johnson.

LBJ firmly believed that he could accomplish anything if he and his adversary could only sit down and talk things over. It worked with Republican Senator Everett Dirksen. The GOP leader with the deep, craggy voice would blast Johnson on the Senate floor, then have a drink the same evening with the president. The two would trade remarks and then make deals so that Johnson's legislation would pass and Dirksen's friends gain political favors. Johnson thought dealing with Ho Chi Minh would work the same way. He failed to realize that Ho was first a revolutionary and second a Communist and that he and the leader of North Vietnam had nothing in common. Ho called the Americans invaders and he refused to take part in any discussions until U.S. forces left Vietnam.

Johnson was more successful with Reverend Martin Luther King, Jr. The African-American civil rights leader came to the White House in 1965 to tell President Johnson that more civil rights legislation was needed. King explained how he intended to go to Selma, Alabama, and lead a march to the state capital in Montgomery. The march, King said, would dramatize the right of blacks to vote. Johnson watched the march on television as Alabama State Police troopers attacked unarmed marchers. The president summoned Alabama's segregationist governor, George Wallace, and told him states rights were fine but the governor had better obey the federal law. He backed up his demands by sending federal troops to protect the marchers from any violence.

Inner Cities Explode

Following the passing of the 1965 Voting Rights Bill, the number of registered black voters went from twenty-nine to fifty-two percent of the population. Aside from bringing many previously unregistered southern blacks to the polling places, however, such dramatic lawmaking had little effect on inner-city blacks. Evidence of their frustration showed in the 1965 Los Angeles riots, started by African-Americans living in the Watts area. There were thirty-four deaths. Property damage, primarily from fires, totaled $200 million. The president could not understand how some black people, who were at last being welcomed into the mainstream of American society, could

National Guardsmen with fixed bayonets push back rioting African-Americans in Detroit's strife-torn west side, July 1967. Troops had been sent in to help police contain the violence; seven thousand people were arrested.

"Our nation is moving toward two societies, one black, one white — separate and unequal."

Kerner Commission report on 1967 race riots

respond by behaving so violently.

Watts was only the first blip on the inner-city racial radar. The summers of 1966, 1967, and 1968 would see rioting in 150 cities, resulting in dozens of deaths and hundreds of millions of dollars lost in burned-up property. The worst rioting took place in Detroit during the last week of July, 1967. At least forty people were killed, two thousand injured and five thousand left homeless. Johnson sent forty-seven hundred paratroopers and eight thousand members of the National Guard to Detroit in an effort to restore order. Ironically, rioting in 1968 was a result of the death of Martin Luther King, Jr., an advocate of nonviolence.

Who were the rioters, and why had the message of pacifism failed to reach them? A National Advisory Commission on Urban Disorders was set up by Johnson. It issued its report in 1968, describing the typical rioter as a male high school dropout who was "nevertheless somewhat better educated than his non-rioting Negro neighbor." Unemployed or underemployed, the rioter was proud of his race yet resentful toward the increasing number of middle-class African-Americans and toward all whites. He knew what the federal commission

"I ran because someone had to do it first. In this country everyone is supposed to be able to run for president, but that's never really been true. I ran because most people think the country isn't ready for a black candidate, not ready for a woman candidate. Someday. . . ."

Shirley Chisholm, educator, congressional representative

Shirley Chisholm.

The first African-American woman elected to the U.S. House of Representatives did it in the turbulent sixties by winning over a majority of voters in her home area of Brooklyn, New York. That woman was Shirley Chisholm.

Chisholm was a Brooklyn native and an honors graduate of Brooklyn College. She also earned a master's degree from Columbia University and was awarded honorary degrees from Talladega College, Hampton Institute, LaSalle College, the University of Maine, and many other colleges and universities. She worked as a nursery school teacher and as an educational consultant before being elected in 1964 to the New York State Assembly.

A Democrat, Chisholm ran successfully for Congress, representing New York's Twelfth District. While a member of the House of Representatives, she also became the first black woman ever to run for president. She did so in 1972, receiving about 1 percent of the vote without appearing on many state ballots. Her campaign centered around women's issues since, she said, "It has always been even harder being a woman than being black."

After her fifteen-year congressional career, during which she wrote two books about politics, Chisholm was a college lecturer in Massachusetts and Georgia. She has been recognized over the years for her work on several issues, including those involving women, children, and African-Americans. A member of the National Association for the Advancement of Colored People (NAACP), Chisholm is important for what she did and when she did it. Progressive America wanted intelligent black women to claim leadership roles, and Chisholm was among the very first to come forward.

By the mid-sixties, many civil rights supporters were being attracted by Black Panther posters like this one, and by charismatic militant speakers such as Stokely Carmichael and Malcolm X, who were talking about "Black Power" and black separatism. The Black Panther Party was formed in California in 1966, mainly to protect the African-American community from police harassment. Although these radicals generally denounced nonviolence as a means to obtain full civil rights, they never inspired the great numbers of followers as had Martin Luther King, Jr. By the end of the decade, the Black Panthers were targeted by the FBI as part of Nixon's conservative policies of law enforcement. A total of twenty-eight Panthers were killed by police in 1969 and a great many more were arrested.

was just finding out: that decades of discrimination in education, employment, and housing had created dangerous people living in deteriorating areas.

It was only a small leap from this attitude to "Black Power," where everything the government tried to do for African-Americans was distrusted. Such an attitude was not new. In the 1920s Marcus Garvey and his "Back to Africa" movement, with its emphasis on black power and pride, was in many ways the forerunner of the Black Muslim movement.

Malcolm X was the most vocal of Black Power leaders, advocating black separatism and militancy. His ideas spread among African-Americans from coast to coast. Leaders such as Huey Newton in Oakland believed part of the solution

> *"It's time for you and me to let the government know it's ballots — or bullets."*
>
> Malcolm X, March 22, 1964

Malcolm X. (1925-1965)

Malcolm X was born in Omaha and named Malcolm Little, the seventh of eleven children. The son of an early political activist who married a West Indian woman of mixed race, Malcolm and his family were run out of Omaha by white vigilantes. In Michigan, a Ku Klux Klan-style terrorist group killed his father. Malcolm dropped out of school in the eighth grade and turned to burglary and other crimes. He was imprisoned for burglary in 1952. While there, he came under the influence of the Islamic religion and began calling himself Malcolm X as his way of rejecting the "Negro slave name" of Little.

Malcolm began educating himself, finding that he was not only capable of immense knowledge but of almost hypnotic speaking power. Following his release from prison, Malcolm's talents earned him the leadership of a mosque (Islamic church) in Harlem in New York City. He rejected the call for the separation of the Nation of Islam (or Black Muslims) from American society, as advocated by the religion's leader at that time, Elijah Mohammed. Instead, Malcolm spoke in favor of an interracial civil war in the United States.

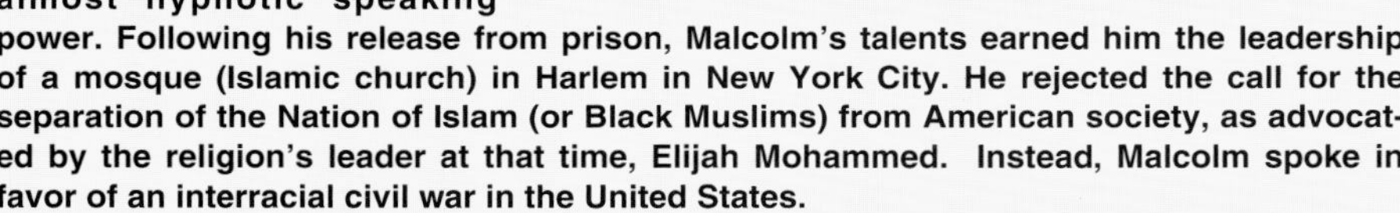

The Muslims expelled him in 1963, and he founded his own organization. Called the Organization of Afro-Americans, it quickly gathered a number of followers, primarily blacks, in northern, urban areas. Malcolm embraced Islam, went on a pilgrimage to Islam's holy shrine of Mecca, won the support of several African and Arab states by his sheer intellect, and denounced Black Muslims as racists.

With a growing international reputation, Malcolm X was seen as a threat to the Nation of Islam. While he slept in February 1965, unidentified firebombers attacked his home. He escaped injury but was assassinated one week later in a New York ballroom while speaking to four hundred followers. Three Black Muslims were convicted of the murder in 1966, though the religion's leaders have always denied involvement.

Neither a total saint nor sinner, Malcolm was idealized after his death. When his *Autobiography* was published in 1966, more people saw him as he really was — a spokesperson for angry, poor, urban African-Americans. He once told inner-city listeners, "America's problem is us."

"We, the black women of today, must accept the full weight of a legacy wrought in blood by our mothers in chains. As heirs to a tradition of perseverance and heroic resistance, we must hasten to take our place wherever our people are forging toward freedom."

Angela Davis, professor and African-American activist

was self defense and he backed his words by issuing rifles. The King assassination and the murder of Black Panther leader Fred Hampton in his bed by a squad of Chicago police in 1969 did nothing to convince militants to set aside their firepower. On the contrary, it only served to increase their desire for self protection. Black students who took over college administration buildings sometimes did so by carrying guns.

The Question of Vietnam

A man of immense energy, Johnson took only a few days off for surgery in 1965 for the removal of his gall bladder and a kidney stone. When the president lifted his shirt to reveal a twelve-inch scar a few weeks after the operation, a political cartoonist drew the incision shaped exactly like Vietnam. At about the same time, Senator Fulbright, Senator Frank Church of Idaho, and others began hearings aimed at questioning the policies that were bringing tragedy to South Vietnam. LBJ responded by getting the Federal Bureau of Investigation to follow antiwar senators around for several weeks.

"End the war! Bring the troops home!" President Johnson could no doubt hear the chants from protesters who picketed every day in front of the White House in 1967. Actually, Johnson could not understand who these protesters were. He was unaware that, with each passing day, more and more Americans believed that waging war in Southeast Asia was wrong. Hawks were becoming doves. Johnson was more concerned, he confided to friends, that the saturation bombing he had ordered over North Vietnam would hit a Soviet or Chinese ship and somehow lead to World War III.

The president tried to speak forcefully about the war. The trouble he had with speaking about the war was that he didn't always tell the truth. Late in 1967, he said that all but 20 percent of the Vietnamese were living under noncommunist rule, thanks to U.S. efforts. Not only was that figure false, it was almost laughable — not even a majority of the South Vietnamese lived under noncommunist rule. Virtually every square foot of South Vietnam belonged to the Viet Cong guerrillas from nightfall to daybreak. The president was a victim of his own "credibility gap": that was the difference between what was said and what was fact. More accurately, Martin Luther King, Jr., pointed out that it was costing the U.S. $322,000 for each enemy killed, compared to an annual federal expenditure of only $53 per person to help Americans below the poverty line. King was reluctant to split with Johnson over the war but was forced to speak out when, in 1967, he said, "The promises of the Great Society have been shot down in the battlefield of Vietnam."

The 1968 Election

Lyndon Johnson had ceased to enjoy his office long before the 1968 presidential election loomed. Johnson was challenged in the Democratic primary that March by Eugene McCarthy, a senator from Minnesota. A witty, decent man, McCarthy decided to take on the president when no one else would challenge the administration's prowar stance. College students who were stirred by McCarthy's principles came to New Hampshire, site of the first presidential primary. They campaigned by the hundreds door-to-door. The senator won 42 percent of the vote, an impressive number against the big bankroll of the established party leader. After Robert Kennedy saw how well McCarthy had done, Kennedy decided he would challenge Johnson, too.

Civil Rights

For further information see primary source entries on pages

11: 1582-83; **12:** 1627-32, 1635-38, 1643-50, 1652-55

Another Assassination, More Violence

More violent tragedies were to strike the nation during election year. Martin Luther King, Jr. went to Memphis in the spring of 1968 to lend moral support to striking garbage workers, most of whom were African-American. He was shot, supposedly by a single gunman, James Earl Ray, an escaped convict who was captured in England a few weeks later. King's father, also a minister, believed that Ray was part of a larger conspiracy and Ray later withdrew his confession.

Despite President Johnson's call for a day of mourning for Dr. King on Sunday, April 7, 1968, many American inner cities erupted in fire and violence. It took more than fifty thousand National Guardsmen and federal troops to restore order in one hundred different cities. Forty-six persons died in the violence, all but five of them black.

Stepping Aside

Johnson hated the thought that he might go down in history as "the mistake between Kennedys." On

Thousands of people followed the mule-drawn wagon carrying the casket of Dr. Martin Luther King, Jr., to Morehouse College for a memorial service and funeral, which was televised nationally. Although King always preached non-violence, his death triggered some of the worst scenes of inner-city rioting, particularly in Memphis, Washington, Baltimore, Chicago, and Pittsburgh.

March 31, 1968, he went on national television to carefully explain the U.S. position in Vietnam. As he neared the end of his thirty-minute talk, Johnson paused before turning his creased and weary face toward the camera once again. In the interest of peace, he said, "I shall not seek and I will not accept another term as your president."

This attempt to bring the country

Robert Kennedy. (1925-1968)

Like many sixties heroes, Robert F. Kennedy was cut down just as he was enjoying his most widespread popularity. A young man with a gun shot him to death on a Los Angeles hotel stage only minutes after Kennedy learned that he had won the California Democratic primary, which could have led to his nomination for the presidency in 1968.

The younger brother of John F. Kennedy, Bobby got his law degree and, because his powerful father was a friend of Republican Senator Joe McCarthy, the new attorney aided McCarthy's persecution of suspected Communists. Bobby distanced himself from the McCarthy hearings, but he found that he liked Washington politics. He became the campaign manager for the winning candidacy of his brother in 1960 and was subsequently named attorney general.

His career as the nation's number one lawman began slowly. He was patient with the aging FBI director, J. Edgar Hoover, perhaps because he knew that Hoover had files on many prominent Democrats. As he learned more about the plight of southern blacks, Kennedy ordered troops into places such as Mississippi and Alabama. But his biggest achievement in forty-four months as attorney general may have been sending James Hoffa, the corrupt head of the Teamsters Union, to federal prison.

Attorney General Robert F. Kennedy, congratulates President Johnson on his address to Congress, November 27, 1963.

Bobby left the attorney general's office in 1964 after drafting the nation's most comprehensive civil rights law. He ran for the U.S. Senate and won easily, representing the state of New York despite the fact that he lived there only briefly. Paying attention to antiwar liberals, he denounced American participation in the Vietnam War, and on March 16, 1968, announced that he was in the running for president.

Bobby Kennedy has been criticized for letting fellow Senator Eugene McCarthy do all of the hard work organizing the antiwar movement, before jumping into the race. Not even Kennedy's closest supporters would deny that he was an opportunist. But he had an uncanny ability to speak to neutral or hostile crowds and win them over. Reporters who followed him through his campaign left their desks damning him and came back enthralled by his ideas.

By June 4, 1968, he had won five of the six primaries he had entered. On June 5, against McCarthy and Hubert Humphrey, Bobby won in California, the most populous state in the nation. As he was speaking at the Ambassador Hotel, he was shot by an Arab immigrant, Sirhan Bishara Sirhan. He died instantly. His untimely death split apart the coalition of migrant workers, African-Americans, Jews, whites, and others who had come together after hearing him speak.

"All the News That's Fit to Print"

The New York Times

LATE CITY EDITION

VOL. CXVII..No. 40,311 — NEW YORK, THURSDAY, JUNE 6, 1968 — 10 CENTS

KENNEDY IS DEAD, VICTIM OF ASSASSIN; SUSPECT, ARAB IMMIGRANT, ARRAIGNED; JOHNSON APPOINTS PANEL ON VIOLENCE

MARCUS TESTIFIES DE SAPIO HAD ROLE IN A CON ED DEAL

Says Itkin Sought Delay of Permit to Aid Own Scheme With Ex-Tammany Head

France Will Meet Tariff Deadline; Strikes Dwindling

By HENRY TANNER

6 IN RACE GUARDED

Secret Service Given Campaign Security Task by President

By MAX FRANKEL

AFTER THE SHOOTING: Senator Kennedy's wife, Ethel, bends over him as a man checks pulse to determine condition

SURGERY IN VAIN

President Calls Death Tragedy, Proclaims a Day of Mourning

By GLADWIN HILL

JERUSALEM POLICE CLASH WITH ARABS

Israelis Halt Procession on Anniversary of War—U.N. Council Meets on Fighting

HANOI INSISTS U.S. HALT ITS BOMBING

Aides Call Talks Response to Johnson—Suspicion Voiced of a Plot Against Kennedy

By HEDRICK SMITH

ROBERT F. KENNEDY

NOTES ON KENNEDY IN SUSPECT'S HOME

Cite 'Necessity' to Murder Senator Before June 5, Anniversary of War

By PETER KIHSS

A Pall Over Politics

Murder Raises Grave Questions for Presidency Races Now and in Future

By TOM WICKER

TRANSIT PACKAGE SUBMITTED TO CITY

M.T.A. Seeks Approval of 8 New Subway Routes

By EMANUEL PERLMUTTER

Italy's Cabinet Quits As Parliament Opens

By ROBERT C. DOTY

Big Board Weighs 4 Special Closings

By VARTANIG G. VARTAN

KUCHEL UNSEATED AS RAFFERTY WINS

Conservative Beats Senator in California's Primary

By LAWRENCE E. DAVIES

Father of Suspect 'Sickened' by News

By TERENCE SMITH

NEWS INDEX

Front page of the New York Times, *June 6, 1968, announcing the assassination of Robert F. Kennedy. No firm conclusions were ever drawn as to the motive for killing this popular political figure, although general opinion was that the assassin, a Palestinian refugee, was striking some kind of blow against Israel.*

together failed. But it did encourage McCarthy, Bobby Kennedy, and the Republican challenger and former vice president, Richard M. Nixon. They all campaigned vigorously, in contrast to Hubert H. Humphrey, who did not enter the primaries. LBJ's vice president became the choice of Democratic party regulars, although it appeared he would have a tough time beating McCarthy and Kennedy in particular.

But Bobby Kennedy was shot, in June, 1968, after having won the California Democratic primary. His killer, Sirhan B. Sirhan, evidently was a deranged loner. The motives of this Palestinian refugee for shooting the presidential candidate were unclear, though Arabs assumed the killing was a blow against Israel. Bobby Kennedy was so well liked by blacks, liberals, and young people that the mourning after his death was almost as widespread as was the mourning for his brother John, assassinated only five years earlier. Bobby Kennedy was laid to rest at the National Cemetery in Arlington, Virginia, in a grave next to his brother's.

President Johnson became more moody and withdrawn than ever following the announcement that he

Eugene J. McCarthy.

Eugene McCarthy studied for the Roman Catholic priesthood for a year before serving in the Army Intelligence in World War II. A high school teacher and then a college economics and sociology instructor, McCarthy won a seat in the U.S. House of Representatives in 1948. The Minnesota Democrat was elected to the U.S. Senate ten years later, where he became an early foe of America's participation in the war in Vietnam. When no other Democrat dared challenge Lyndon Johnson in the 1968 presidential campaign, McCarthy decided to run.

He became an instant favorite with college students, who left school for days at a time so they could campaign door-to-door for McCarthy in early primary elections. "Stay clean for Gene" became their watchwords. McCarthy won 40 percent of the Democratic vote in the first primary, held in New Hampshire. Johnson's narrow margin of victory against an unknown Senator with little money played a part in the president deciding not to seek reelection.

The senator's candidacy brought together many small groups that opposed the war, giving these groups strength in numbers. More important, voicing his concerns about the war gave many fellow Democrats the courage to balk at American warmaking.

McCarthy's early success prompted Bobby Kennedy to enter the race. But by the time of Kennedy's death in June, Hubert Humphrey had won the backing of too many regular Democrats for McCarthy to be nominated as the party's candidate. At the infamous 1968 Democratic convention, McCarthy backers who were congregating peacefully in the streets were beaten by Chicago police, who also invaded McCarthy headquarters. McCarthy did not seek reelection to the Senate in 1970.

An intellectual, McCarthy has written fifteen books on a wide range of topics, from politics to poetry. He called 1968 "the hard year," and has since run for the office of president several times without success. His campaign showed politicians in both parties that enthusiastic volunteers could be as effective as money in winning over the minds of voters.

George Wallace.

To his admirers, he was a bantam rooster spoiling for a fight, eager to defend the rights of ordinary forgotten Americans. To his enemies, he was a loudmouth who stood in the way not only of progress but of law and order. There were plenty of Americans rooting for and against George Corley Wallace.

George Wallace was a demagogue — he gained power by appealing to the prejudices of the people. He was also a populist — a politician who wanted to represent the average citizen. An amateur boxer, he was elected the governor of Alabama in 1962. Not primarily a racial segregationist, Wallace latched on to segregation when he saw that it reflected the views of voters, most of whom were white at the time.

The governor made history by standing in the door of the University of Alabama, refusing to admit African-American students. Federal troops had to be called to integrate the college. Afterward, he spoke at many colleges. Students nearly always disrupted him, which made him more popular with more conservative Americans. His popularity increased as he criticized any kind of protestor, particularly those who were liberal or radical.

Running for president in 1968, Wallace found it hard to outflank Republican Richard Nixon on the law-and-order issue. His own vice presidential running mate was former Air Force General Curtis LeMay, who said in his first news conference that the "most efficient" thing to do in Vietnam was to drop nuclear weapons! Despite these and other mistakes on the part of his colleague, Wallace managed to earn the support of 9.9 million voters, or 13.5 percent of all votes cast.

The 1968 election was to be his last. Wallace was shot by Arthur Bremer, a deranged follower, while he campaigned for office in 1972. The Alabaman has, since then, been paralyzed from the waist down and has remained in constant pain. Several years after his final run for office, Wallace said he had been wrong to stand in the way of progress by black Americans.

"If this nation can afford to spend $30 billion to put a man on the moon, it can afford what it takes to put a man on his feet here on earth."

Hubert Humphrey, 1968

would not seek reelection. There was an unspoken feeling that any campaigning he might do for Humphrey would only damage the vice president's chances against Nixon in the fall. Adding to LBJ's sorrows, the Democratic convention in Chicago in August turned into a police riot, as hippies and activists were chased and beaten by Chicago police while protesting in parks and on city streets. Mainstream Democrats became worried about the people who were supporting Gene McCarthy. Johnson had hoped his bowing out would heal wounds. As he could see, the war was infecting his political party and the entire country.

There were many more Democrats than Republicans in the

country at the time. The majority in both parties appeared to support the war. They were opposed by the young, by most minorities, by intellectuals, and by many in the clergy. The last year of Johnson's presidency saw many parents and children cease to speak to each other over the war. It saw parishioners walk out of churches in the middle of antiwar sermons. It saw the police, who were symbols of authority, become objects of hate, especially among big-city blacks. Even though peace talks began three days after Johnson's refusal to seek reelection, the war dragged on and on.

Hubert Humphrey never said so in public, but many people suspected that loyalty to Lyndon Johnson prevented him from abandoning a prowar stance. Numerous liberals and activists, shouting "Dump the Hump," decided to sit out the 1968 race. Lyndon Johnson kept a low profile, telling an aide that being a lame duck president was like being "caught in an endless nightmare." On election day, Richard Nixon was able to take advantage of the white backlash and received 43 percent of the vote, Hubert Humphrey 42 percent, and George Wallace of Alabama 15 percent. Johnson's turn at America's helm ended, and the Texan returned to his home.

Wallace had no hope of winning the election, but he had grabbed voters from the Democrats and the Republicans, making him a key figure. The two major candidates each pulled more than thirty-one million votes. The Alabama governor earned the vote of 9.9 million Americans. Who were these people? Wallace craftily played both sides of the fence over the war, saying that he would never send U.S. troops to battle and then prevent them from winning. Such a statement could be construed as either anti- or prowar, depending on the listener's interpretation. Many Wallace voters were against racial integration and disapproved of demonstrations. Richard Nixon's vice president, Spiro Agnew, would soon pick up the popular law-and-order theme and run with it.

Nixon as President

Richard M. Nixon was among the stranger persons ever to seek the office of president. Shy to the point that he had trouble looking people in the eye, he nonetheless repeatedly sought political office. Elected to Congress and to the Senate as a rabid anticommunist, he campaigned and was chosen as vice president to Dwight Eisenhower in 1952. During his two terms under Ike, he frequently attacked Democrats, questioning their loyalty to the country. In 1960, Nixon lost one of the closest presidential races ever to Democrat John F. Kennedy.

"The new leadership will end the war . . . and win the peace."

Richard M.Nixon

That slowed him only for the moment. In 1962, he ran for governor of California and was surprised that he lost. But he could not stay away from politics and so spent much of the sixties supporting fellow Republicans and doing other political favors. When he entered the Republican primary for the presidency in 1968, few were surprised.

The new president said during the campaign that he had a secret plan for ending U.S. involvement in Vietnam, but he never revealed it until after he was elected. Then he began to with-

Presidential candidate Richard Nixon flourishes a double victory salute at the Republican National Convention, August 8, 1968, to the cheers and applause of delegates and spectators. He promised that his administration would bring the people together.

draw U.S. troops from Southeast Asia in a program termed *Vietnamization* — letting the South Vietnamese shoulder more and more of the fighting. Despite this program, the conflict soon became Nixon's war. He and his national security advisor, Henry Kissinger, approved widening the war without congressional authorization by approving the invasion of Cambodia in search of Communist hideouts. This gave new life to the antiwar movement and, in 1972, caused Democrats to support peace candidate Senator George McGovern.

Less than one week before the signing of an agreement in 1973 to end U.S. participation in the war,

Lyndon Johnson suffered a heart attack at his ranch and was pronounced dead on arrival at a San Antonio hospital. A close friend said he, in fact, smoked, drank, and brooded himself to death as he thought constantly of recent history. He was 64 years old.

Appraising the Johnson Years

Clearly, Johnson believed the country could support a costly war and expensive social programs at the same time. To do this, he relied on deficit spending, in other words, spending more on federal programs than he received through federal taxes and other income. In his last year of office, Johnson's deficit ran at around $25 billion.

There were problems with the U.S. economy during the 1960s, but recession was not one of them. The president was able to keep the country artificially prosperous by gearing it for war. Defense plants scoured the country for talented people to hire. Wages climbed because workers with skills or experience were in great demand. Union members took advantage of the situation by successfully negotiating major improvements in pay and benefits — even though their productivity did not increase. And since no one wanted to hire young men who would soon be sent to war, many entry-level jobs went unfilled.

The U.S. labor force expanded, too. There were 65,778,000 employed adults in 1960 and 78,678,000 ten years later. Those unemployed were 3,852,000 and 4,093,000, respectively. That means the rate of unemployment went down, from 5.5 percent to 4.9 percent, because the total number of people in the workforce grew. The percentage of workers in labor unions went down, too, from 31.4 percent in 1960 to 27.3 percent in 1970. Despite their continued decline, unions led the fight to buy American-made goods.

The agricultural economy also changed. The number of farms declined from about five million in 1960 to approximately 3.5 million in 1970. The size of the average farm grew, from 297 acres in 1960, to 374 ten years later. The percentage of workers in farm occupations during the decade dropped from 6.1 percent to 3.6 percent of the U.S. workforce. Yet crop production from those farms edged ever upward.

As the smaller farmers sold out to the larger farmers, those remaining took advantage of government subsidies and price supports to earn a good living. The Federal Department of Agriculture, with the blessings of both Democrats and Republicans, followed New Deal policies in actually paying farmers not to grow crops for which there were surpluses. Such programs have survived budget cuts to this day.

Unfortunately for Johnson, the Vietnam war proved too heavy a drain on the nation's resources. As a result, most of his Great Society programs remained underfunded. However, two measures of its success are that the percentage of impoverished Americans fell to 12 percent in 1969, compared to 22 percent in 1959, while the Civil Rights Acts of 1964 and 1965 changed the lives of African-Americans for ever. The greatest weakness of the Great Society was that it promised more than any government could possibly hope to deliver.

CHAPTER 4
Whither the American Dream?

Veterans from World War II with their families waiting to take possession of their newly built homes in Queens, New York, in 1954. Some of these young children would grow up to become the rebellious teenagers of the sixties — the "baby boom" generation destined to "Turn on, tune in, drop out."

The Dream Turns Sour

To many white, middle-class, and middle-aged Americans who had experienced the Great Depression and seen a world ravaged by war, the postwar era must have seemed like a dream fulfilled. They had comfortable, suburban homes, good schools for their children, plenty of food on the table, one, two or more cars in the garage, and secure neighborhoods and communities.

Baby boom children enjoyed a standard of living and educational opportunities unprecedented in American history. They had music lessons, became Brownies, Girl and Boy Scouts, joined Little League teams and were constantly entertained by the television. Popular TV heroes

like the Lone Ranger, Lassie, and Rin-Tin-Tin portrayed good as always prevailing over evil and everything seemed right with the world.

By the 1960s, however, the baby boomers had become young adults and some began to cast doubts on aspects of the suburban dream lifestyle that had previously gone more or less unquestioned. If life was so good, why was the threat of nuclear war hanging over their heads all the time? Why were their black brothers and sisters still denied many basic human rights? Why did happiness seem to rely on conforming to the suburban lifestyle and embracing the value systems of their parents?

At the same time, among the nation's minorities, there blossomed the notion of ethnic identity. Blacks, Hispanics, American Indians, and others began to take pride in their race and culture and sought to gain the recognition and status they truly deserved.

Since the mid-fifties a great many African-Americans had been steadily increasing their demands for equal status with whites. As we have seen, the 1960s brought a continuation of the struggle, with great new leaders emerging, like Martin Luther King, Jr., Malcolm X, and others. But other groups were also joining the fight and claiming their share of the dream.

Hispanic-Americans

One of the least reported but most important trends during the decade was the increase in size and importance of the country's Hispanic population. Just three million Hispanic-Americans existed in 1960. Ten years later, the figure had tripled. They came not only from Mexico but from Puerto Rico, the rest of the Caribbean, and Central and South America. Few ethnic groups showed up and succeeded as quickly as the Cubans did.

Only three thousand Cubans had left immediately in 1959 when Fidel Castro became leader. That number grew to 155,000 by 1962, and many of the refugees settled in Miami. They brought money and skills and often prospered, joining the Republican party by the late 1960s to show their opposition to Castro's communism. Though they left friends behind, they could look to successes in their new country, such as baseball player Tony Oliva of the Minnesota Twins or salsa singer Celiz Cruz.

Other Hispanics making names for themselves included Puerto Ricans such as ballplayers Orlando Cepeda of the San Francisco Giants and Roberto Clemente, the Hall of Fame outfielder for the Pittsburgh Pirates; a professional golfer Juan "Chi-Chi" Rodriguez; Tito Puente, a graduate of the exclusive Juilliard School of Music in New York and a bandleader; playwright Rene Marquis; and Rita Moreno, winner of the 1962 Oscar for Best Supporting Actress in the movie version of *West Side Story*. Many Puerto Ricans emigrated to New York City, while Mexican-Americans settled in the Southwest and in California.

They include everyone from singers Linda Ronstadt to Vikki Carr, from Congressman Eligio de la Garza to Senator Joseph Montoya, from rocker Ritchie Valens to tennis star Richard "Pancho" Gonzalez, from golf pro Lee Trevino to singer-activist Joan Baez, and from actors Ricardo Montalban to Anthony Quinn. These

IMMIGRATION

For further information see primary source entries on pages

11: 1454-60, 1484-85, 1490-91, 1514-16;
12: 1696-98, 1715-17

people — who shared the Spanish language and culture, and a strong loyalty to their family and community — became a major influence.

Many Hispanics, especially in the West, became citizens automatically in 1966, thanks to an amnesty that made them legal residents, but there were many issues remaining to be settled.

These included the bracero problem, which involved migrant laborers brought in from Mexico to work in poor conditions and for low wages, especially in areas where the local Hispanic-American workers were beginning to organize into unions.

Additionally, there were many undocumented immigrants, especially from Mexico, who had crossed the 2,000-mile border illegally. They were exploited both by the guides who brought them into the country and by the employers who hired them for slave wages. Even those Hispanic-Americans who were in the country legally faced discrimination from employers, and long after the Brown decision in 1954, some schools and other public facilities in the Southwest remained segregated. Furthermore, because Hispanic-Americans were considered to be "white," they did not receive many of the legal protections afforded to other minorities.

Not all Hispanic-Americans shared the same vision for their peo-

LABOR

For further information see primary source entries on pages

11: 1478-79, 1485-88, 1535-37; **12:** 1655-57

César Chávez. (1927-1993)

Early in the decade in California, a Mexican-American named César Chávez formed a union of migrant farm workers, the United Farm Workers Association. These homeless people made only about $2,000 a year; there was work no more than six or seven months each year; and fringe benefits for them and their children did not exist. The first migrant workers to strike were the grape pickers, who staged a work stoppage in Delano, California, in 1965.

Chávez was forty-one at the time. He had begun work as a migrant laborer and for ten years had worked in a community organization, where he learned how to organize people. By 1966, Chávez had attracted many supporters among civil rights workers and peace activists and had begun the largest strike by farm workers in the history of California. His targets were the state's big vineyards.

Chávez won the support of the American Federation of Labor-Congress of Industrial Organizations (AFL-CIO, a group of unions) early in his fight. Other sympathizers included churches nationwide who convinced many members to boycott buying and eating grapes. Grape growers insisted on using some 350,000 Mexicans with California work permits. Chávez pointed out that the growers were blatantly using the poorest people in Mexico in an attempt to defeat the poorest people in the United States.

The labor leader went on a twenty-five-day fast that permanently affected his health. But in March, 1966, with the help of sympathizers, he won the first real contract for migrant workers in the history of the American labor movement. In the middle of 1970, ten of the largest growers negotiated contracts with the union. Since then, Chávez and his followers have won rights for lettuce pickers and others who travel from one harvest to the next.

Chávez remained close to the movement he founded and served as president of the United Farm Workers until his death in 1993.

The law by which Mexican immigrants could be brought into the U.S., mostly to work as poorly paid farmhands, expired at the end of 1964. This was despite the protests of growers and farmers who employed the "braceroes," (meaning hands) as they were known, to work long hours doing tedious work like berry picking for very little money.

ple. César Chávez, leader of the United Farm Workers Association, believed that Hispanic-Americans should assimilate into American society, while former boxer, successful businessman, playwright, and poet Rodolfo "Corky" Gonzales felt that they should take pride in their separateness. To some extent this diversity of opinions reflected the diversity of origins of the Hispanic-American peoples.

They were united for the most part, however, in realizing that the key to economic power lay in gaining political power and influence, especially in those regions where Hispanic-Americans formed the majority. Against the odds, Hispanic-American Henry B. Gonzales was elected Democratic representative of San Antonio, Texas, in 1961. In 1964 Texans elected E. "Kika" del la Garza as representative of the Lower Rio Grande River. By 1970, José Angel Gutiérrez had formed the pressure group, La Raza Unida, which roughly translates into "the people united."

American Indians

The cultural identity of the American Indians remained threatened throughout the sixties, despite the political developments of the previous three decades. While the Hispanic-Americans were finding a voice, American Indians were fighting for their land rights in the courts. By the 1960s, two-thirds of all American Indians lived off reservations, mostly in large cities. They had little say in the running of the reservations, which were managed by the Bureau of Indian Affairs.

But whether they resided on the reservation or off, the American Indians were without doubt the most disadvantaged of all the country's many ethnic and racial minorities. Unemployment could be as high as 50 percent and the school dropout rate was about the same. Around 38 percent lived below the poverty line, compared to 33 percent of African-Americans and 12 percent of America's population as a whole. Life expectancy was forty-six years, compared to the national average of sixty-nine years. They were more prone to serious illnesses like tuberculosis, alcoholism was rife, and the suicide rate was twice the national average.

American Indians were organizing, however. They met, both on the reservations and off, to discuss their needs, persuaded some museums to return sacred objects that had been stolen from their lands, and sued to reclaim land, water, and other rights they had lost when treaties were ignored or broken.

Some joined more militant groups to try to achieve social reform by force. Others resorted to the courts, via the Indian Claims Commission (ICC), a body set up by President Truman in 1946 to settle grievances against the government. During its thirty-two-year lifetime, the ICC awarded about $775 million to Native American claimants and heard 670 cases. In 1978, it was dissolved and its work taken over by the U.S. Court of Claims.

> *"The problem that has no name — which is simply the fact that American women are kept from growing to their full human capacities — is taking a far greater toll on the physical and mental health of our country than any known disease."*
>
> Betty Friedan, *The Feminine Mystique*

What Role for Women?

In October of 1963, a Presidential Commission on the Status of Women, which had been set up by President Kennedy in 1961, issued its report. First chaired by Eleanor Roosevelt, and then by Esther Peterson, it identified many of the issues that would occupy feminists over the following decades, providing statistics on the position of

The National Women's Liberation Movement campaigned hard to encourage a more positive attitude towards women as free-thinking individuals. In 1968, demonstrators picketed the Miss America Pageant, which they believed symbolic of brainless beauties parading purely for the gratification of men.

By the start of the decade, the big cities were being continually adapted for an increasing volume of highway traffic. This picture shows the James Lick Highway in San Francisco, as it was in 1960.

be dreadful — until mild, mechanical air came along. By the sixties, there were many people who were never away from dependable central air conditioning. Comfort, lower housing prices, and job opportunities caused increasing numbers of northerners to visit and then settle in the southern tier of the United States.

What is mobility without a car? Not much, most Americans believed then as now. The most popular car of the sixties was the small, sleek Ford Mustang, introduced in 1964 as a convertible and also as a two-door sedan. The squared-off, mid-size automobile was available with a six-cylinder engine or a more thirsty and

Top of the range automobiles developed a sleeker profile and a more aero-dynamic design to reach higher speeds, a smarter finish, and a safer, more comfortable ride. The Ford Mustang fastback with new accent stripe was introduced in 1968.

powerful V-8. Everyone from girl-chasing bachelors to empty nesters (those whose children had left the home) bought the zippy cars. Lee Iacocca, the man who guided the Mustang into production, later left the Ford Motor Company to take over the troubled Chrysler Corporation.

The Population Bulge

Elementary and secondary school enrollment reached forty-five million children during the 1969-1970 academic year. That was nine million more than a decade before and four million more than would be enrolled during the 1979-1980 year. The average school term grew to more than 178 days; every school district had to build new schools as split-day teaching (with shifts of students attending school at different times) became the only way to educate all the nation's children. At about this same time, scores on achievement tests peaked and began to decline. Why?

Many inside and outside education would blame the radicalism of the 1960s. Radicals wanted history, for example, to be relevant to student's everyday lives, not just a set of dates and acts of Congress. A current university professor who was teaching then says he remembers those students fondly. "They were interested in the process of education," is how he recalls them.

Teachers were looked to more and more for stability. Their training included "intervention," picking up on signs of neglect, poverty, or hunger and alerting school or local authorities. Because the number of births declined later in the 1960s and because many young men studied to be teachers to avoid military service, a surplus of teachers arose. Besides improving the quality of teaching by giving every school district a huge selection of teachers, the surplus kept salaries down. If a teacher asked for too much money, another candidate stood waiting in the wings. Teachers' pay failed to keep up with the wages and salaries of many other occupations, not all of which required as many years of study to acquire college degrees as teaching did.

More Sex and Violence

In classrooms, in homes, and on the streets, Americans became more violent. Richard M. Nixon may have been guilty of exaggeration at times during his 1968 law-and-order campaign. But he was not stretching the truth when he told crowds everywhere that there were nine times as many crimes being reported than there were during the Eisenhower administration of the 1950s.

Increasingly, violence involved gun use. By the end of the decade, cities such as Chicago, Detroit, and Washington, D.C., were averaging three violent deaths a day, the vast majority of them the results of handgun shootings. Most often, the assailant and the victim knew each other, leading authorities to believe that a handgun kept in a home or apartment would sooner or later be used on a resident of that dwelling. The other trend showed that minorities were disproportionately involved in this gunplay, both as assailants and victims. Vice President Spiro Agnew railed for law and order but did not call for the elimination of handguns.

Young people, who were such a large percentage of the population, lost much of the respect they had for authority. No longer did children automatically obey teachers, law enforcement personnel, or their parents. Kids rationalized; they told each other, "Never trust anyone over thirty." One of the reasons things got so out of hand may have been that adults lied to their children, and the children saw through the lies.

Among those who failed to tell Americans the truth were Lyndon Johnson, and virtually every member of his administration, when they spoke of Vietnam. In addition, adults told young people that marijuana would kill them. When they tried it and had no such dire effects, the young people ceased to believe any drug warnings. African-Americans were told anything to keep them from rioting, and they knew it. Small wonder that, as the decade passed, they listened less to the nonviolent Reverend Martin Luther King, Jr., and more to Black Power spokesman Stokely Carmichael, who advocated that African-Americans should arm themselves.

To further confuse and disgust adults, hippies and their followers talked about new standards of beauty. They shrugged off appearance, labeling people beautiful if they were pleasant, fun, or intelligent. Many were also indiscriminate about sex. Consequently, the birth control pill may have prevented many unwanted pregnancies, but it helped spread disease by making sex seem a no-risk proposition. Incidences of syphilis and gonorrhea skyrocketed among the young. Gonorrhea was contracted by thousands of U.S. servicemen in Vietnam, and forms of syphilis that resisted penicillin worried health authorities.

Television began to cover such frank subjects more often, but did so in shorter and shorter segments. TV became the source for the instant opinion, the sweeping generalization, and the rash summary. Despite more government programs than ever, problems actually seemed to grow. A cynic at the time felt more accurate statistical surveys were the best thing to come from governmental sources. What television did with that data was something else again.

> *"The youth rebellion is a worldwide phenomenon that has not been seen in history. I do not believe they will calm down and be ad execs at thirty as the Establishment would like us to believe."*
>
> William Burroughs, author of the *Naked Lunch*

CHAPTER 5
The Counterculture Blooms

The ingredients that would go into the counterculture were cooking in the Bay area of northern California in 1965. A longtime center of Beatnik activity, San Francisco also was the home of several explosive new rock 'n' roll bands: Jefferson Airplane, Big Brother and the Holding Company, and The Grateful Dead, among others. Across the bay in Oakland, Black Power activists began to organize. At the Port of Oakland, young soldiers were shipped off by the thousands as part of the troop buildup in Vietnam. North of Oakland was Berkeley and the University of California. This massive campus, with its longtime radical community, had been the site of antiwar, freedom of speech, and other protests for several years. The underground press helped bring these and other flashes of energy together.

The "Summer of Love" began in Golden Gate Park, San Francisco, with the Monterey pop festival, in June 1967. Around 50,000 young people enjoyed the music of The Beatles, Otis Redding, Ravi Shankar, the Mamas and the Papas, Janis Joplin, Jimi Hendrix, and other great rock stars of the time. Later, thousands more flocked to the city seeking that festival atmosphere and San Francisco became a "hippie haven."

Underground News

Underground or alternative newspapers were born even before the sixties began. The first such newspaper to find conservatives and liberals equally uninteresting was the *Village Voice*, introduced in the fall of 1955. The weekly offered news of Greenwich Village in New York City, providing a very personal kind of journalism. It covered events and the arts and offered frequently unpopular or unusual opinions. In the next few years would come the *Realist* and the *East Village Other* in New York, the *Free Press* in Los Angeles, and the *Barb* in Berkeley, California.

These publications, and as many as five hundred other underground newspapers, had a few things in common. They were outrageous, politically provocative, sometimes obscene and totally biased. Young people loved them. Distributed free or sold for a quarter or less, the papers told where the latest antiwar protest would be, where popular bands were playing, whether undercover police were looking for drug users, and how to find low-cost food, health care, or a place to sleep.

As circulation increased, the publications became more specialized. Some devoted their space strictly to music, while others pursued counterculture themes and were printed in explosions of color and psychedelic (hallucination-like) design. Still others remained politically hard-core, damning mainstream leaders and the war. Most, though, mixed the themes of sex, drugs, and rock 'n' roll.

By 1968, the papers and their poorly paid writers, editors, artists, and photographers were being imitated by major publications. Advertising agencies picked up on the colorful look of the underground papers and used vibrant colors to sell everything from cars to political candidates. Many of the papers subscribed to Liberation News Service (LNS), an underground version of the Associated Press. LNS gathered news from its subscriber newspapers and passed it along in regular mailings. At their peak, underground papers were read by as many as four million radicals, hippies, minorities, soldiers, advertising copywriters — and law enforcement personnel.

Alternative news hit its peak in 1969. Afterward, many women would quit reading the alternative newspapers because they had become feminists and they found a lot there to dislike. Females who were hippies or radicals grew tired of being known only as somebody's "old lady." Did they not have personalities, ideas, and lives of their own? Women also objected to being portrayed as sex objects. And record companies, which had advertised heavily in the alternative press, were scared off by police and the Federal Bureau of Investigation. In 1969, the San Francisco office of the FBI and the CIA, which by law should not operate domestically, put pressure on CBS, owners of Columbia Records at the time. Soon Columbia ads began to disappear from the underground press. A CIA statement of January 1969 suggested that, should any record companies choose to advertise in the underground press, they would be considered as giving "aid and comfort to enemies of the United States."

Many of the most talented writers and editors ran out of energy or

"The Youth International Revolution will begin with a mass breakdown of authority.... Tribes of long hairs, blacks, armed women, workers, peasants and students will take over.... The White House will become one big commune.... The Pentagon will be replaced with an LSD experimental farm.... To steal from the rich is a sacred and religious act."

Jerry Rubin in his book *Do It*

became completely alienated. Headlines such as "Enemy [meaning the U.S.] bombs Hanoi," showed that some alternative newspeople had given up hope for America. And no one could live forever on the meager pay the papers handed out. A few, however, such as *Rolling Stone*, not only survived but prospered. Those papers that survived beyond the sixties turned their attention to local news, to entertainment and show business, or simply to better, more thoughtful, and more balanced writing within their pages.

Trouble on the Campuses

"We are people of this generation, bred in at least modest comfort, housed now in universities, looking uncomfortably to the world we inherit." So began the fifty-page Port Huron statement, issued in June 1962 by sixty members of the Students for a Democratic Society (SDS), a radical student movement formed by a small group of students at the University of Michigan in 1960.

The SDS formed the core of the New Left, a political movement disillusioned with liberal politics, which believed that war and racism could only be eradicated by fundamental change in American society.

One of the first open signs of the emergent student protest movement came on the Berkeley campus of the University of California in the fall of 1964. Nervous college officials had banned on-campus recruitment for off-campus political activities. The free speech banner was one that the radical students could unite around. On December 2, nearly 6,000 students gathered to listen to speeches and to folk singer Joan Baez perform "We shall overcome." Eventually, university officials backed down, lifting the ban early in 1965. But by then student protest had spread to campuses across the nation.

In April 1968, around 5,000 students, led by the SDS and the Students' Afro-American Society, staged a takeover of the University of Columbia in New York City. They were protesting the placement of a new gymnasium in an adjacent black area — seen as a "racist" symbol of the university's total disregard for African-American neighborhoods — and the university's links to the Institute for Defense Analysis, which was considered to be aiding the Vietnam War. The takeover ended after a week, when 1,000 police officers ended the students' actions.

Who were these new revolutionaries, prepared to take on their teachers and college officials? For the most part, they were the white sons and daughters of the middle class. The GI Bill of Rights of 1944 and the National Defense Education Act of 1958 gave young people unprecedented educational opportunities. During the fifties and sixties, college numbers swelled from around one million in 1950 to nearly eight million by the end of the sixties. Growing up in economic security, these young people could afford to be rebellious and idealistic. Under President Kennedy they joined the Peace Corps and VISTA, got involved in the civil rights movement, and were the freedom riders of 1961. Under President Johnson, they later also turned their attention to protesting the war in Vietnam.

Though they formed the minority

"And yet where in your history books is the tale of the genocide basic to this country's birth? of the preachers who lied? how the Bill of Rights failed."

Buffy Sainte-Marie, singer, "My Country 'Tis of Thy People You're Dying," 1966

on campus (probably fewer than 12 percent of students joined in with their radical activities) these New Left members were vocal and made themselves heard across the nation. Advocating "participatory democracy," they were against what they saw as the massive government, educational and corporate institutions that stifled individual freedoms and left ordinary people powerless. As we shall see, their later involvement in the antiwar movement was a factor leading finally to the U.S. disengaging itself from the war in Vietnam.

Spreading the Word

The counterculture popped up simultaneously in different locations nationwide because of the America's transportation and telecommunications networks and media coverage. Interstate highways connected all major cities by the end of the 1960s, while airlines did the same thing, only much faster and at greater altitude. A rock band or an activist could do something silly or new or important one day and show up some three

About 5,000 students camped out for a week in front of the Low Memorial Library on the Columbia University campus in 1968 to protest what they saw as the university's racism and links to the military. It took 1,000 police officers to end the demonstration, which was one of the most publicized protests of the decade. Some 700 people were arrested and 148 injured in the confrontation.

Janis Joplin. (1943-1970)

From outcast to superstar to martyr — more than one person followed that road in the 1960s. Among them was Janis Joplin.

She was born in the oil-port city of Port Arthur, Texas, growing up amid people who saw themselves as average Americans. In high school in the late fifties, Janis Joplin was all but spat on. She was ugly, she dressed unconventionally, and she shared few interests with her classmates.

As soon as she graduated from high school, Joplin headed for the West Coast. In San Francisco she began to sing with an amateurish group of rock musicians. Together they were known as Big Brother and the Holding Company. Joplin's gut-wrenching versions of old blues and new rock gained her immediate local fame. She appeared at several rock festivals and overwhelmed the crowd with her gutsy singing style. Soon, she was known nationally and internationally.

Dressed funkily, she did exactly what she pleased, singing as she drank Southern Comfort, a sweetened whiskey, on-stage. She owned dozens of outlandish costumes and a sports car painted in psychedelic colors. "If I miss," she told a reporter, "I'll never have a second chance on nothing. But I gotta risk it. I never hold back, man. I'm always on the outer limits of probability."

Despite warnings that her performances would cause an early ruin of her vocal cords, she continued. Joplin's voice on such songs as "Bobby McGee," "Piece of My Heart," "Ball and Chain," and "Summertime" earned her an entire generation of fans. But she lived very much as she acted on stage, and she seriously abused drugs. She died of a drug overdose in 1970, but not before she returned in triumph one last time to her high school's class reunion in Port Arthur, Texas.

thousand miles away in person to tell others all about it the next. Some bands and musicians, traveling by plane or in large and swanky buses, were able to crisscross the country for a series of concerts that involved tens of millions of dollars.

Grace Slick, lead singer of Jefferson Airplane, is said to have wandered barefoot into a California automobile showroom in order to look at a new, exotic Ferrari. A salesman in a suit and a tie emerged from the office to shoo her away — before she reached into her well-worn jeans and began to bring forth $1,000 bills. If rockers were rich, some were spoiled, too. Major stars would spend time between appearances holed up in an exclusive hotel's most expensive suites. Some, like members of the British group, The Who, would then often vandalize the accommodations. Bands insisted on and got huge limousines, police escorts, and catered meals backstage before, during, or following performances.

The Fashion World Explodes

The young people of the counterculture frowned on anything that represented the status quo and their dress reflected this. Out was the neat, orderly attire of the previous generation. In were headbands, earrings, jewelry, sunglasses, boots, sandals, bell-bottom pants, and frilly shirts that exploded with color and designs. Clothes were decorated with fringes and patches and men's clothing was as colorful as women's. Loose-flowing ethnic (especially Asian Indian and African) and second hand clothes were popular. Men wore beads, grew giant sideburns, and let their hair grow long in the most defiant fashion change of the decade, and often the most frequent cause of antagonism between boys and their parents. Women and girls wore their hair longer — sometimes using an iron on it for the desired straight appearance.

"Turn on, Tune in, Drop Out"

The essence of the counterculture was the rejection of the "Establishment" — the prevailing middle-class attitudes, values and beliefs, the political system, and the institutions of the nation that represented authority and power.

Science and technology were blamed for leading the world to the brink of nuclear annihilation, so the counterculture stressed the need to return to the simple life. "Doing your own thing" replaced doing what you were told for many free-thinkers.

Timothy Leary was one self-appointed "guru" of many drug-using members of the counterculture. He experimented with LSD and, by violating a pledge not to involve any of his undergraduates in this, was fired from Harvard University. He coined the slogan "Turn on, tune in, drop out" to characterize his philosophy. The use of LSD declined when some of its various harmful side-effects were discovered, such as "bad trips" and possible genetic disorders.

Former Harvard University professor Timothy Leary addressed the National Student Association conference in 1967 advocating use of the mind-altering drug LSD, and declaring that its legalization was inevitable.

Other threats to the counterculture resulted from its attractiveness for some people who were deranged — or worse. Late in 1969, Sharon Tate, a pregnant Hollywood actress, and four of her house guests were brutally murdered in a wealthy Los Angeles suburb. Charles Manson had rounded up a group of nine girls and five boys and led them south to an old ranch in the California desert. Manson had already spent seven years in prison, and, using mysticism and drugs, he proved that flower children weren't just victims but would victimize if given the opportunity. A few days after the Tate murders, these obscure hippies were arrested. Manson never admitted that he had directed the killing, but several members of his "family" told police that they had been involved.

"Won't You Please Come to Chicago?"

When politics mixed with the counterculture, strange and sometimes frightening things took place. The first hint of trouble may have come in 1967, when the National Conference for New Politics took place on Labor Day weekend in Chicago. Representatives of radical and pacifist causes met with African-Americans and carefree people who may have liked the idea of "revolution for the hell of it." Martin Luther King, Jr., the keynote speaker, was interrupted by Black Power advocates chanting "Kill whitey!" Black militants produced anti-Israel and anti-Jewish platforms, and many whites at the conference gave them votes of support — even though numerous radicals and pacifists were Jews.

A supercoalition of all these groups, with all their different aims, made little sense. That was evident a few weeks later, when antiwar advocates staged the March on Washington. Demonstrators were overwhelmingly white and liberals or pacifists. To African-Americans, there were things more important than the war. Organizations such as the SDS also began to break up as individual members became Marxists, nonviolent hippies, commune-dwelling hermits, or yippies.

Yippies, members of the Youth International Party, were an unstructured bunch that included former political activists such as Abbie Hoffman and Jerry Rubin. The yippies called for a "Festival of Life" in the streets of Chicago during the Democratic National Convention in 1968, to contrast with the "Festival of Death" inside the convention hall. Yippies were against conventional power relations and sought to use theatrics to unmask this power. They intended to overthrow the government by talking dirty, having sex in public, and generally making noise. Also planning to be in Chicago were members of the more conventional and serious National Mobilization to End the War in Vietnam.

Opposed to anyone but regular Democratic conventioneers was Chicago's mayor, Richard J. Daley. Yippies and their ragtag friends began making outrageous statements and provoking worried questions weeks before the convention. Would they put LSD in the drinking water? Would they seduce Democratic wives? Mayor Daley and his political machine were being whipped into a fury. They didn't see a handful of clowns; instead, they viewed the yippies as the leading edge of rebellion and anarchy. Presidential candidate Eugene McCarthy felt the atmosphere tense in Chicago and told his supporters to stay home.

What happened in the streets of Chicago in August 1968 has been called "a police riot." All protesters, from the most wild-eyed yippie to

"As long as I am Mayor, there will be law and order in Chicago."

Mayor Richard J. Daley, 1968

the most sincere member of the clergy, were viewed by law enforcement as the same. When they marched after being denied a parade permit, many were beaten senseless, then arrested. Huge numbers of people — reporters, photographers, onlookers, undercover FBI personnel, convention delegates — were bullied or battered by Chicago police. There were six hundred arrests. One-third of those arrested required medical attention. The police, some of whom had suffered cut knuckles in the altercations, even raided the McCarthy headquarters.

The event was, of course, broadcast live all across the country. Patrons in bars squared off, some siding with the police and others backing the demonstrators. Families shouted at each other above the din from the TV set, antiwar children snapping at their law-and-order parents. Conventioneers watched Mayor Daley shaking his fist and yelling obscenities at delegates who deplored the police repression. When the streets cleared of people and tear gas and the convention ended, eight protesters stood accused of conspiring to cause a riot.

Called the "Chicago Seven," though there were, in fact, eight, they were: Abbie Hoffman and Jerry Rubin, founders of the yippie movement; David Dellinger, a middle-aged pacifist; Bobby Seale of the militant

Four of the chief delegates to the National Conference for New Politics in Chicago, 1967, were, from left to right: prominent pediatrician Benjamin Spock; Rev. Ralph Abernathy, aide to Dr. King; entertainer Dick Gregory; and Dr. Martin Luther King, Jr. Their attempt to form a new political group was not successful.

Abbie Hoffman. (1936-1989)

The difference between most revolutionaries and the yippies, founded by Abbie Hoffman, was that the yippies were "revolutionary artists. . . [whose] concept of revolution is that it is fun." In a decade that took itself very seriously, everybody needed Abbie Hoffman and his occasionally disgusting and obscene ideas of having a good time.

Hoffman was born in Worcester, Massachusetts, the son of a pharmacist and a housewife. His first brush with radicalism may have occurred at Brandeis University, from which he graduated in 1959. The highlight of his years as an undergraduate, he said, was hearing Fidel Castro speak at nearby Harvard University.

Abbie (a nickname for Abbott) went to graduate school in psychology at the University of California, Berkeley, a school with a long radical tradition. Hoffman participated in a demonstration against the House Un-American Activities Committee, then toured with a film of the HUAC hearings. Sponsored by the American Civil Liberties Union, he spoke of 142 factual errors in the government-created film.

Hoffman took over a Massachusetts chapter of the National Association for the Advancement of Colored People (NAACP), becoming deeply involved in politics and racial issues. His experiences there were followed in 1964 by joining the Student Nonviolent Coordinating Committee (SNCC) and heading south to protest racial segregation. By mid-1965, he was fired from his regular job as a pharmaceuticals sales representative and was using marijuana and even taking LSD.

At several points in his life, Hoffman decided having fun was more important than acting his age. He went to New York to join emerging hippies, got involved in street theater and protested any number of things. In 1967, at an antiwar rally in Washington, he met Jerry Rubin as Rubin was attempting to levitate the Pentagon! The two soon formed the Youth International Party or yippies and announced plans to perform at the 1968 Democratic convention in Chicago.

Hoffman was arrested approximately ten times between the summer of 1968 and the following summer. He was charged with everything from desecrating the flag to inciting a riot. Somehow, Hoffman found the money and time to visit Woodstock, meet with attorney William Kunstler, and plan an ambitious tour of colleges to be well paid for making speeches.

He also was one of the many people who "brought the war home," agitating constantly in the United States as American GIs continued to be sent to Vietnam. Unfortunately, he was thirty-four by 1970. When he told kids never to trust anyone over the age of thirty, it had a certain false ring. Hoffman left the country briefly to avoid being arrested, taking his children and second wife to the Caribbean. Hoffman lived from 1974 to 1980 in upstate New York, hiding from the law.

After serving a brief prison sentence, Abbie Hoffman found the 1980s stifling. He committed suicide in 1989.

Black Panthers; Tom Hayden and Rennie Davis of SDS; and John Froines and Lee Weiner, radical professors. Although they all held beliefs well to the left of the political center, the defendants didn't have much else in common. They were tried in Judge Julius Hoffman's Chicago courtroom, and they made a joke of the proceedings in various ways. At one point, Bobby Seale was bound and gagged, then sentenced to four years in prison

Ten thousand antiwar demonstrators, mostly white liberals or pacifists, marched on Chicago in August, 1968, during the Democratic National Convention. They were met and easily outnumbered by a 20,000-strong force of police, by National Guardsmen, and soldiers, who injured many hundreds of protestors resulting in public outrage. Out of six hundred people arrested, a third needed some kind of medical treatment.

by the elderly judge for contempt of court. Froines and Weiner were found innocent of all charges, and the others served little or no time after years of appeals.

The "Silent Majority" Prevails

Although he failed to win a majority of all votes, Richard Nixon's election was seen by at least some Americans as a relief. It seemed that enough people longed for a conventional president in such unconventional times to see him elected. In his 1968 election campaign Nixon had pledged to fight for the "Silent majority" and listen to "the great majority of Americans, the forgotten Americans, the non-shouters, the non-demonstrators." By collecting together a coalition of traditional conservative Republicans and former southern Democrats disillusioned with liberal politics, he sought to move the country to the right, away from the Great Society and towards individual responsibility.

With Nixon's election, antiwar Americans and others on the left knew who their enemy was and Americans on the right could rally behind the new president. After the events of 1968, things got quieter, despite Vice President Spiro Agnew's snarling at the media and at intellectuals. Besides being Nixon's attack dog, Agnew recruited George Wallace backers with each speech. Neither Agnew nor Wallace would figure in national politics after the early seventies. Arthur Bremer shot Wallace as he campaigned for the 1972 presidential election. Agnew took a bribe while governor of Maryland, and, as a result, was forced to resign the vice presidency in 1973 after the details of the indiscretion were exposed publicly.

The Beat Goes On

By decade's end, with many of their heroes dead or imprisoned, and their hopes for peace and a new social order in America shattered, young people's interest in the counterculture began to subside. But the music that had accompanied the movement lived on. Rock 'n' roll sprang up all over the place. In East Los Angeles, Mexican-Americans were dancing to the guitar licks of Santana. In college towns such as Austin, Texas, and Madison, Wisconsin, concerts by the famous and not-so-famous were used to raise money, feed the homeless, and most of all, to entertain. Southern rockers, who had started it all, played towns such as Athens, Georgia, and Chapel Hill, North Carolina. Live, electric, and well-performed rock and roll, folk rock, and pure folk music was everywhere.

Jimi Hendrix. (1942-1970)

Hendrix was born Johnny Allen Hendrix in Seattle. A left-handed player who took up the guitar at the age of twelve, he used right-handed instruments played upside down. He also experimented with extreme levels of feedback and reverberation to create entirely new sounds from his electrified instruments.

By 1963, Hendrix was a respected recording-session guitarist. Three years later, he formed a blues band called "Jimmy James and the Blue Flames." Shortly afterward, Hendrix moved to England and put together a new group, the "Jimi Hendrix Experience," with British players Noel Redding on bass and Mitch Mitchell on drums.

British audiences loved American blues, and Hendrix laid it on them heavily. He played soul music and his own tunes, blending unique sounds with showmanship and destruction. Hendrix played the guitar with his teeth and behind his back, often ending a concert by setting his instrument on fire. Eric Clapton, Peter Townshend, and several heavy-metal bands of the 1970s were strongly influenced by him.

As his stage performances got wilder, so did his personal life. He wore incredible psychedelic clothing and put on roaring performances that left his music ringing in the ears of fans for hours. Hendrix played "The National Anthem" at Woodstock in 1969 on his guitar in such a way that the hundreds of thousands of fans were left in stunned silence. Songs such as "Purple Haze," "All Along the Watch Tower," and "Hey Joe" are considered classics. But behind the frantic behavior and immense talent was almost continuous drug use.

Hendrix died in 1970 of barbiturate intoxication in London while on a European tour. He was twenty-seven years old.

CHAPTER 6
American Interests: the World Outside

Life as we know it came close to ending in October 1962. The United States and the Soviet Union both possessed nuclear weapons. They very nearly used these and other weapons on each other, an event that could have blotted out all humans, animals, and plant life on earth. The story begins with a Communist revolution in America's backyard.

A Modern Revolutionary

In 1953, Fidel Castro Ruz began to organize a revolution in Cuba. A Roman Catholic law graduate, Castro was the illegitimate son of a middle-class native of Spain and his Cuban cook. Sickened by the repression and corruption of the country's dictator, General Fulgencio Batista, Castro led an unsuccessful attack on an army barracks that landed him in jail for two years. When he got out in 1955, he went to Mexico to reorganize his followers. The Castroites returned to Cuba in 1956, but were chased into the Sierra Maestra mountains after trying without success to stage an invasion. From their mountain stronghold, Castro and his followers gradually took control of most of the country.

The Cuban government finally fell when Batista fled the country on New Year's Eve, 1958. Castro named himself prime minister two months later. Then, he took on the responsibilities of commander-in-chief of the armed forces and head of the nation's only political party. In 1960, he allied himself with the Soviet Union, and in 1961, he publicly declared that he was a Communist.

The reality of a Communist nation ninety miles from American shores frightened many Americans. In 1960, Eisenhower ordered a 700,000-ton cut in sugar imports from Cuba. A year later, the administration broke off diplomatic relations with Cuba altogether. Castro seemed to take great pleasure in ending trade with the United States and grabbing property held by American companies and Cuban anticommunists. All this served to anger the United States Government, particularly those branches involved in spying and sabotage. The CIA trained, paid, and provided arms for fourteen hundred Cubans to stage a military invasion in 1961. These anti-Castro Cubans landed in an area known as the Bay of Pigs. Those who were not killed by Castro's troops were quickly imprisoned. John F. Kennedy, president only three months when the calamity took place, told the press, "Victory has 100 fathers and defeat is an orphan." The ill-planned invasion made the new chief executive look as if his administration was inept. In contrast, Cubans celebrated, staging parades to honor Castro.

Psychedelic-style posters of Cuban heroes Fidel Castro and Che Guevara were hugely popular among young American radicals in the 1960s, particularly after the death of Guevara, who was considered a martyr for his cause.

A Wall and Weapons

That same summer, Kennedy met Soviet Premier Nikita Khrushchev in Vienna. They did not get along — the two men were visibly tense and hostile toward each other. Krushchev threatened to cut Berlin off from the rest of Europe, and Kennedy reminded the Soviet leader of the U.S.' tactical weapon strength. After World War II, Germany had been divided into democratic West Germany and Communist East Germany. Berlin, similarly divided into eastern and western zones, was situated in the middle of East Germany. Its allied-controlled western zone was therefore isolated from West Germany and the rest of western Europe. Khrushchev built a wall between East and West Berlin, and Kennedy called up troops to show that he was serious about keeping the former German capital open. Robert McNamara, secretary of defense, told reporters, "We will use nuclear weapons wherever and whenever to protect our national interests."

The chance to aim missiles at each other came quickly. The Soviets began sending technicians and advisors to Cuba, followed by weapons and supplies. The Soviet Union at the time had only six missiles capable of reaching the United States, compared to hundreds of American missiles

President Kennedy was given the opportunity to look over the wall dividing East and West Berlin via a specially erected platform during his ten-day visit to Europe in June, 1963. The wall was built to stop East Germans from escaping to the West, and became a solid symbol of Communist repression.

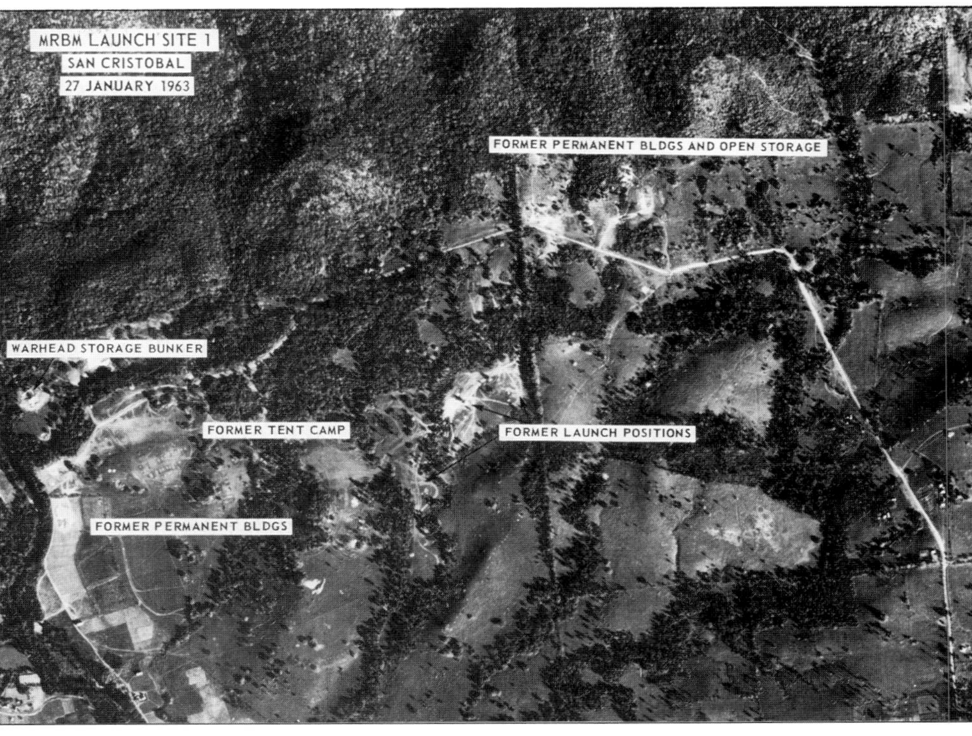

The event that almost sparked World War III — the Cuban Missile Crisis. Early in 1963, Defense Secretary Robert McNamara sent this photograph to Senator Kenneth B. Keating as proof that the Soviets had begun dismantling the missile launch sites in Cuba. It had been taken using the latest aerial reconnaissance techniques.

aimed at the Soviets from Turkey, Italy, and elsewhere. Khrushchev was further goaded by the Chinese, who called him soft on America. The Soviet premier became obsessed with the possibility that Cuba might be invaded by the United States and thus lost to communism.

On October 14, 1962, an American spy plane flew over Cuba and took pictures of several thirty-foot long, medium-range missiles capable of hitting half of the cities in the United States. Kennedy advisors knew that the missiles were both a military and a political threat. Besides endangering citizens, the Cuban weapons would diminish the stature of the United States in the eyes of other governments. The president's people suggested destroying the weapons with a quick air strike or staging a naval blockade to prevent more missiles from arriving in Cuba. Kennedy, remembering the Bay of Pigs, said only that the United States had to do something that was more carefully planned.

"We do not want to fight — but we have fought before."

John F. Kennedy on Berlin, before the wall went up.

Bigger, Better Missiles

Before a decision could be made, additional flights over Cuba revealed a new base with missiles that could hit 98 percent of the United States. Kennedy ordered the navy to blockade all Soviet ships carrying arms. He also ordered ground troops to be ready. In a spell-binding television address on the evening of October 22, the president told of "a series of offensive missile sites" in Cuba and warned darkly that the United States would retaliate on the Soviet Union directly if any missiles were fired from Cuba toward the United States.

The Soviets felt Kennedy was employing a double standard. If the United States could point missiles at

Moscow from Turkey, why couldn't the USSR point missiles at Washington from Cuba? Castro, who felt that his country was being used by both superpowers, nevertheless readied one hundred thousand troops for a U.S. invasion. The U.S. Strategic Air Command put fifty-seven B-52 bombers in the air, ready to fly with deadly nuclear bombs toward the Soviet Union. Some civilians in Washington, New York, and elsewhere emptied store shelves of food for emergency use or else fled into the countryside.

The U.S. Navy took America to the very brink of war by dropping small depth charge explosives into Caribbean waters that forced six Soviet submarines to surface. Some Soviet ships stopped dead in the water, awaiting orders from Moscow. President Kennedy so feared a war that he told the navy not to fire upon Soviet ships unless he himself gave a direct order. At that point, there were forty-two offensive missiles and atomic warheads already on the island. Neither Kennedy nor any of his staff knew that Soviet commanders in

Nuclear Age

For further information see primary source entries on pages

11: 1565-67; **12:** 1651-52, 1666-69, 1690-92, 1698-1700

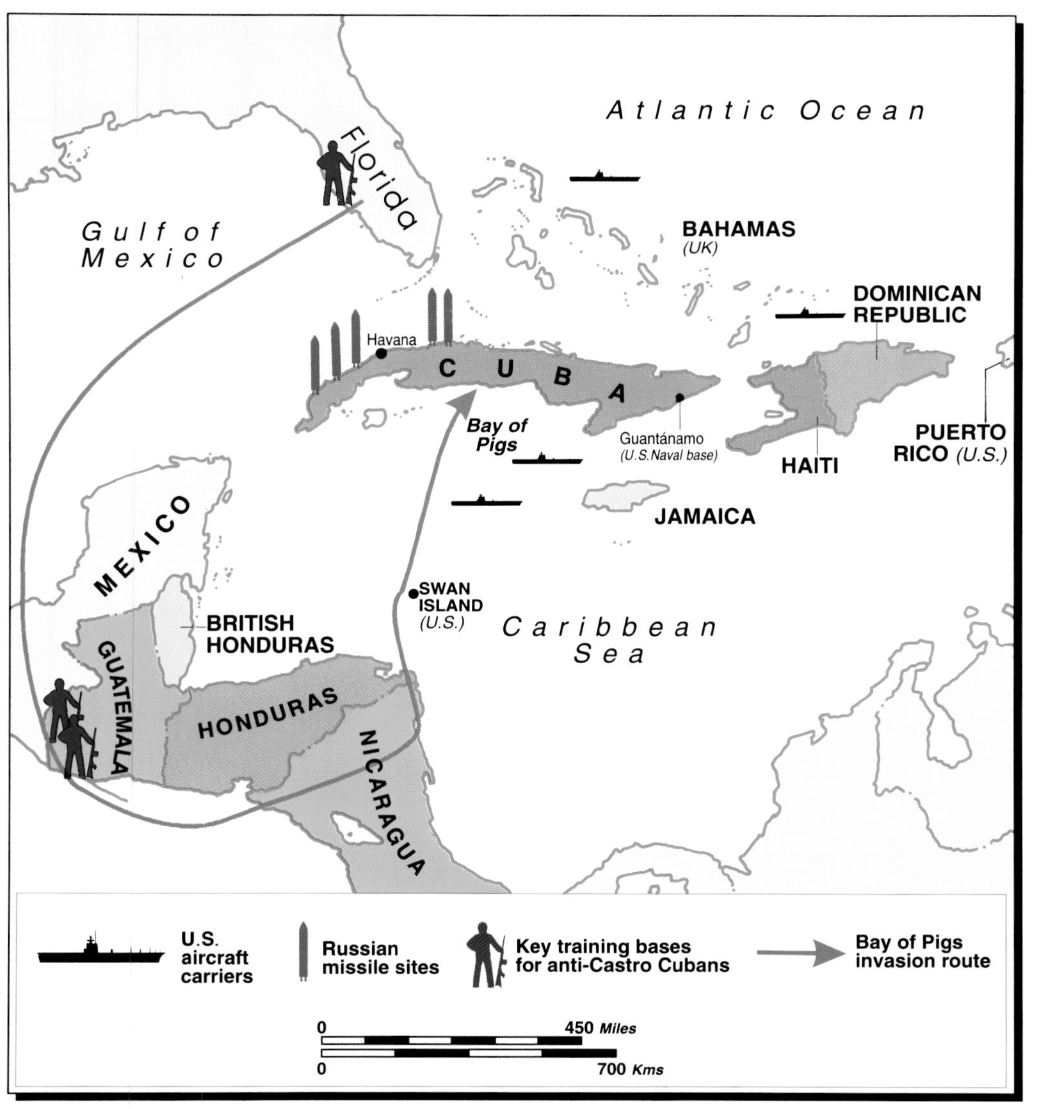

Cuba represented a Communist stronghold rather too close to home. Only ninety miles from American terrain, the United States government felt compelled to interfere in that country's affairs — in 1961 with the ill-fated American-backed Bay of Pigs invasion, and in 1962 when war seemed imminent over the Cuban missile crisis.

> *"Esteemed Mr. President.... I understand very well your anxiety.... In order to liquidate with greater speed the dangerous conflict,... the Soviet government... has issued an order for the dismantling of weapons, which you describe as 'offensive,' their crating, and return to the Soviet Union.... The U.N. may verify the dismantling.... Respectfully yours, Nikita Khrushchev."*
>
> Nikita Khrushchev to President Kennedy, 1962

Cuba had been given the authority to fire their missiles at the United States as they saw fit!

Back at United Nations headquarters in New York, the U.S. ambassador, Adlai Stevenson, asked his Soviet counterpart whether he could deny there were offensive missiles in Cuba, aimed at the U.S. mainland. The Soviet, Andrei Gromyko, said that he was in no hurry to answer. "I am not in an American court," he said through a translator. "I am prepared to wait for your answer until hell freezes over," Stevenson replied.

On October 26, Kennedy and his advisors received a teletype message that both frightened them and gave them hope. It was from Nikita Khrushchev, and it was written with tremendous emotion. The Soviet leader voiced fears and concerns, but also showed he was grimly determined not to back down in front of a world that was watching. He said he would remove the missiles if the United States vowed never to invade Cuba. The Americans read and reread the message, wondering if Khrushchev might crack under the strain of possible destruction.

The next day, as demonstrators insisted that the crisis be resolved, Khrushchev sent a second, tougher message. He said the crisis would go away only if the United States promised never to invade Cuba and if American missiles were removed from Turkey. Kennedy, advised by his brother, Bobby, replied to the first message, but ignored the second. He pledged that the U.S. would never invade Cuba. At the same time, he ordered 250,000 troops on alert in Georgia, in Florida, and on the base at Guantánamo, Cuba, a small land parcel kept throughout the Castro revolution by the U.S. Navy. Finally, on October 28, Khrushchev backed down and the world breathed again.

After two weeks of crisis, President Kennedy went to Mass at a church near the White House. A friend nodded to the president as they went inside, and Kennedy said, "This morning we have an extra reason to pray." The Cuban missile crisis, as it came to be known, was the last time Soviets and Americans threatened each other while "gazing down the nuclear gun barrel," as one presidential aide said.

Civil Wars

All over the world in the 1960s there were a number of civil wars. Most involved native people attempting to overthrow dictators or to force colonial authorities to leave land the people considered theirs. The United States often ended up on one side and the Soviets on the other in these confrontations. Most involved a group of guerrillas, armed by one or more Communist nations, against either a European power or against that power's designated government. Places as different as India, Yemen, Zaire, Ghana, Indonesia, and the island of Cyprus saw strife.

Africa in the 1960s became a source of interest to many black Americans. All over the huge continent, European colonies were becoming independent countries. African leaders began to make headlines as countries like Uganda and Kenya, experimented with independence.

Following the missile crisis, Castro tried to export Cuba's revolutionary ideology to several countries in the 1960s. Cuba's most notorious supporter of guerrilla wars was a man named Ernesto "Che" Guevara. Born in Argentina, Guevara overcame severe asthma to become an athlete and a scholar. His published writings called for anti-colonial wars of liberation and he became something of a hero among young radicals. Travels as a student in South America convinced him that the United States was behind many of the undemocratic military dictatorships he saw and disliked there.

He joined Castro in 1956, becoming a military leader. After the overthrow of the Batista government in 1959, Guevara became a Cuban citizen and represented his newly adopted country abroad.

After 1965, Guevara dropped out of sight. Rumors said he was disappointed in Cuba's slow economic progress, or that he wanted to deal with the Chinese rather than the Soviets for aid. Except for a mysterious letter calling for all-out war against imperialism, the revolutionary's whereabouts were not known. He surfaced in Bolivia in 1967, and on October 8 of that year, was captured with a group of rebels who were part of a special Bolivian army unit. The thirty-nine-year-old Communist was shot shortly afterward. Young people in the United States and elsewhere protested his death, and Guevara became a martyr to many of the world's leftists.

But Whose Land Is It?

The state of Israel was created, with the backing of the Truman administration, by the United Nations in 1948 from parts of Palestine, a predominantly Muslim country. America's 4.3 million practicing Jews and others gave money and lent political influence and moral

Israeli troops in Jerusalem on their way to capture the biblical city of Jericho, June 7, 1967. They smashed through Arab forces in Jordan, seizing most of the area west of the Jordan river, including the historic city. This prompted a call for "permanent peace" in the Middle East.

support to Israel. The founding of Israel created thousands of Palestinian refugees, and fomented extreme hostility between Israel and its allies and many of the surrounding Arab states.

The United States saw Israel throughout the 1960s as a consistent ally in an area that had been historically unstable. Several times in the last fifty years, wars have been fought over which group — Arab, Israeli, or other — has the right to live on this disputed land. One of the most intense conflicts took place in 1967, following a decade of fierce unresolved dispute.

The Six-day War

Angered over the blockading of the Israeli port of Elat by the Soviet-backed Egyptian Navy under President Nasser, the Israelis attacked their neighbor without warning on June 5, 1967. Armed with the latest American and other western equipment, they blasted Egypt's airfields, knocking out virtually all of Nasser's planes as they sat on the ground. In the Sinai Desert, Israeli tanks and troops killed an estimated ten thousand Egyptians, reaching the Suez Canal on June 9. For good measure, the Israelis also captured pieces of Syria and Jordan. Egypt was crushed and Nasser resigned. The canal became a dividing line between two enemy camps as a result of what is now known as the Six-day War.

"We are committed to defying any attempt to destroy Israel, whatever the source."

Bobby Kennedy in California, June 1, 1968

Israel's lightning-like military success wasn't lost on Americans, who had been evaluating their own war in Vietnam. They saw on television that Israel's tough minister of defense, Moshe Dayan, wore a patch over his left eye, which was lost fighting for his country. Eye patches in all shapes and sizes were sent to Robert McNamara, the U.S. secretary of defense, in the hope that they might somehow magically aid his attempt to rout the Viet Cong from South Vietnam!

Israel now occupied a huge chunk of Egyptian land, the Sinai desert. The United States and the Soviet Union pressured Israel and Egypt to sit down and negotiate in 1970 but the negotiations failed.

Other Warring Neighbors

The United States was at least as worried about China during the 1960s as it was about the Soviet Union. China — with close to nine hundred million people — was considered unpredictable and well armed with an atomic bomb. The Chinese also seemed unable to get along with their neighbors for any period of time. Equally frightening, China was furnishing the North Vietnamese with weapons and, U.S. officials feared, might launch an attack if U.S. planes strayed into Chinese airspace or hit a Chinese ship in the North Vietnamese harbor of Haiphong.

Successive U.S administrations continued to distrust the Chinese. Anticommunism was still prevalent, and there were U.S. interests to protect in Guam, Japan, Taiwan, and the Philippines. But, as the decade drew to a close, the Chinese hinted that they might want to re-establish diplomatic relations with the United States. This secret suggestion, at the height of America's war with Vietnam, would be explored in the 1970s by Richard Nixon.

The U.S. government feared Communist China as much as they did the Soviet Union. Chinese leader Mao Zedong reviewing his army in 1963 from Tienanmen Gate.

Strained Relations

America's relations with its traditional allies and with neighbors closer to home were continually tested throughout the decade. In Central America, Panamanians wanted to control the American-dug canal that, since 1914, had allowed ships to travel between the Atlantic and Pacific oceans. America had always operated the canal, but riots in Panama in 1964 led to a proposal for a new canal treaty. America acted as nobly in Panama as it acted badly in the Dominican Republic.

East of Cuba in the Caribbean Sea, the Dominican Republic shares a large island with Haiti. The country was run from 1930 to 1961 by an American ally and brutal dictator, General Rafael Leonidas Trujillo Molina. After Molina's assassination in 1961, Juan Bosch was elected president but overthrown in 1963.

A revolt staged in 1965 by Bosch's followers and some Communists was broken up after only four days by U.S. Marines, ordered to the Dominican Republic by Lyndon Johnson. Several Americans in and out of government pointed out that by in effect declaring war in another country without congressional approval, Johnson acted without regard to the U.S. Constitution. There was talk, but only in left-wing intellectual circles, of trying to impeach LBJ. Regardless, the intrusion into another country's politics by the United States did not make America more popular abroad.

Nor did the Vietnam War. Several of America's staunchest allies distanced themselves from the United States at the height of the war. Canada permitted draft dodgers — people who left the United States to avoid military service — to live there. Other havens for pacifists and AWOL U.S. soldiers included the Scandinavian countries. Charles DeGaulle, the premier of France at the time, withdrew French forces from the North Atlantic Treaty Organization (NATO) command in 1966, partly in protest over the war. DeGaulle also constantly criticized the United States for actions taken in Vietnam. Great Britain's government repeatedly tried to resolve the war in Vietnam, while British citizens demonstrated against America's military presence in Southeast Asia.

As the decade drew to a close, there was unrest in South America. In Chile, the government had been grabbing foreign-owned mining interests for several years. Americans, who owned some of the mines, assumed they would be paid or that the mines would be returned —

U.S. troops patrolling the streets of Santo Domingo, Dominican Republic, in September, 1965, were heckled by groups of women showing their resentment of U.S. intervention by clapping their hands and shouting "Go home Yankee." Fearing the Dominican Republic might become another Cuba if left in the hands of Juan Bosch, Lyndon Johnson sent in the U.S. Marines.

until a Marxist was freely elected in 1970. His name was Salvador Allende Gossens. Nixon objected to Allende's take over of American owned businesses and was concerned that Chile might develop stronger ties with Cuba and the Soviet Union. In 1973, Allende was overthrown and killed by a group of military leaders who together had vowed to "exterminate Marxism." America's CIA assisted the generals in subverting Allende's government.

This was by no means the first attempt by the CIA to destabilize or directly overthrow a foreign government. We have already seen how they were unsuccessful in their 1961 attempt to overthrow Castro. They were involved in the assassination of the leader of the Congo, in Africa, in 1953. That same year, they overthrew the Iranian government of Dr. Mohammed Mossadegh. A year later, they successfully overthrew the government of Guatemala, but were unsuccessful in their attempt to unseat the Indonesian government in 1957.

The Rise of the Multinationals

While American governments continued to intervene in the politics of other countries, a quieter, but by no means less consequential, overseas invasion was also taking place — by American corporations. The Marshall Plan of 1948 had sought to stabilize and revitalize European economies. But it had other aims. Among them was to create a network of American corporate control around the globe, while building up export markets for American goods.

Throughout the fifties and sixties, American corporations penetrated the international economy, successfully setting up subsidiary companies in many countries on a scale never seen before. These corporations were called multinationals, but at that time most of the top executives in the overseas subsidiaries of such companies were actually American citizens.

By the early seventies, about 300 U.S. corporations, including the seven largest banks, earned altogether something like 40 percent of their profits outside of the country. At that time they were growing at a rate two or three times faster than the U.S. economy as a whole. After the United States and Soviet Union, these huge multinationals constituted, as a group, the third largest economy in the world.

The most profitable places to set up shop were developing countries, where labor was cheap and commercial, and environmental regulations very lax. Between 1950 and 1965, U.S. corporations invested $1.8 billion in Europe and reaped a total of $5.5 billion in profits. Over the same period they invested $3.8 billion in Latin America and profited to the tune of $14.3 billion.

These huge multinationals were able to exert great influence over foreign policy. Especially powerful were the oil corporations. The so-called "Seven Sisters" — Exxon, Mobil, So-Cal, Texaco, Gulf, Royal Dutch Shell, and British Petroleum — pursued policies that quickly depleted the American oil supply and forced U.S. dependence on exported oil, especially from the Middle East. This was to have dire consequences during the seventies and eighties.

CHAPTER 7
Vietnam: War Without End

> *"There's a consensus out that it's OK to kill when your government decides who to kill. If you kill inside the country you get in trouble. If you kill outside the country, right time, right season, latest enemy, you get a medal."*
>
> Joan Baez, singer

"We had to destroy the village to save it."

So said a weary young U.S. Army officer after a battle with enemy soldiers in Vietnam in 1968. His words sum up America's experience in that war-torn country. Everything the United States did in the Southeast Asian nation seemed to go wrong. President Eisenhower dreaded a land war, yet he sent advisors to train South Vietnam's army. President Kennedy spoke of peace but increased the number of advisors there and gave the South Vietnamese well-armed helicopters and other weapons.

South Vietnamese troops, assisted by their American advisor, negotiate a muddy river after the bloody battle of Ap Bac, 1965.

President Johnson inherited a limited war with the presidency and chose to expand it.

No U.S. president wanted South Vietnam to be overrun by its close Communist neighbor, North Vietnam. Vietnam had been split into separate Communist and noncommunist countries in a 1954 peace agreement and, in 1955, Ngo Dinh Diem came to power in the south. He was a staunch Roman Catholic, fiercely anticommunist, and a ruthless dictator. He immediately appointed his

Buddhist monks pray outside the National Palace in Saigon as an expression of their disapproval of the war in October, 1967.

VIETNAM WAR

For further information see primary source entries on pages

12: 1638-43, 1660-63

brother head of the secret police and led a harsh and corrupt regime that was very unpopular. Diem promised to hold a reuniting election in 1956. But the South Vietnamese, supported by the U.S., cancelled the election because they feared that the winner would be a northern Communist, Ho Chi Minh. Ho was a veteran anti-colonialist who had fought for a Communist Vietnam since the 1930s. After the aborted election, guerrilla activity against the government began immediately. South Vietnamese guerrillas, later called Viet Cong, were armed and aided by northern soldiers.

Meanwhile, Diem had failed to keep promises of land reform, and ruthlessly persecuted and killed hundreds of Buddhists, who, he alleged, were assisting the Communists. In 1963, a military coup, backed by the CIA, resulted in his overthrow. He was assassinated on November 2 of that year.

Guerrilla Warfare

At about the time that Dwight Eisenhower handed the U.S. government over to John Kennedy on January 20, 1961, the Viet Cong began random, sneak attacks on American bases and buildings. At first, the guerrillas would not confront U.S. soldiers in the open. Instead, they set off powerful bombs that ripped through army barracks or reduced offices, shops, and bars to hunks of glass, concrete, and metal.

John Kennedy's advisors wanted him to be aggressive in Vietnam. Kennedy stalled them, but, in 1964, they were able to persuade the next president, Lyndon Johnson, that sending more troops was the right idea. In March 1965, Johnson ordered marines into Vietnam. Their assignment was to defend the big U.S. Air Force base at Danang. Additional troops were sent soon afterward, as the government and the military of South Vietnam both proved to be weak and corrupt. George Ball, undersecretary of state, was the only Johnson advisor who immediately advocated a pullout. Ball wanted to walk away and let the corrupt Saigon government fall. But he was overruled by Secretary of Defense Robert McNamara and by Secretary of State Dean Rusk.

American forces were needed because South Vietnam's Army of the Republic of Vietnam (ARVN) troops were poorly trained soldiers. Although some were brave, many mistreated civilians, tortured prisoners, and ran from danger. In a telling battle in 1963, hundreds of heavily armed ARVN soldiers surrounded a small Viet Cong unit in what was called the battle of Ap Bac. But the guerrillas shot the south's soldiers to pieces and escaped. American advisors told government officials in Washington of the event, and some began to wonder about further U.S. involvement.

How was it that one South Vietnamese behaved badly as an ARVN soldier while another fought bravely as a Viet Cong? Many ARVN troops were trained by wealthy Vietnamese who bribed officials to keep them away from any fighting. The young soldiers were issued the latest weapons but did not always know how to use, clean, or repair them. Above all, most had no idea why they were fighting. The Viet Cong fought for a reunited, Communist-led Vietnam. They saw

American troops as invaders and South Vietnamese troops as mere American puppets.

By mid-1964, there were twenty-one thousand American soldiers in South Vietnam. There were advisors in and near the cities and Green Beret units in villages along the western border with Cambodia and Laos. The Green Berets trained mountain tribes-people to spy and to resist the Viet Cong and North Vietnamese. They also brought medicine and improved sanitation. Fighting in and around these lonely outposts in the early 1960s amounted to a secret jungle war, unknown to most Americans.

The conflict in Asia made headlines on August 4, 1964. A U.S. Navy destroyer, the *Maddox*, came under mysterious attack in bad weather off the coast of North Vietnam. The captain reported being fired upon by three enemy ships in the Gulf of Tonkin. The *Maddox* returned fire, and there were no injuries. Before the captain determined that no enemy boats were actually seen, President Johnson ordered a counterattack. He sent sixty-four U.S. Navy jets into North Vietnam to bomb oil tanks and ships. The aircraft were met by heavy fire; two planes were shot down, and one pilot was taken prisoner. The president asked Congress to pass the Gulf of Tonkin Resolution. The quickly approved measure gave the president many of the same powers as

U.S. Navy jets take off from their carrier ship during the Gulf of Tonkin incident, August 1964. Out of sixty-four jets sent to bomb oil tanks and ships, two were shot down and one pilot was taken prisoner.

an actual declaration of war. The Tonkin incident, it later transpired, was largely a pretext for Johnson to intervene in Vietnam. He had been carrying the request in his back pocket for some time, just waiting for the right moment.

Troop Buildup Begins

Large numbers of U.S. troops were sent to South Vietnam in 1965 under General William Westmoreland. He faced the task of uniting the South Vietnamese, teaching them defense, and directing his own forces in a land of mountains, jungles, and rice paddies. Westmoreland stayed out of Vietnamese politics, though he and others saw Buddhist priests lead demonstrations to protest the fact that most Vietnamese had no voice in the government. In the United States, television viewers turned away in horror as the orange-robed Buddhist priests protested by soaking themselves with gasoline and lighting a match to erupt in a ball of fire.

William Westmoreland.

Tall, handsome, and from South Carolina, where the military tradition is strong, General William C. Westmoreland was a West Point graduate. He served in World War II and in the Korean conflict, showing heroism and leadership in both wars. He seemed a wise choice to head American troops in Vietnam in 1964.

Once chosen, the general immediately asked for more soldiers, telling his bosses in Washington that the war would be over sooner if additional manpower were available. During the four years that followed, Westmoreland usually got what he asked for in terms of men and equipment. Yet American deaths increased while little progress was made.

Westmoreland tried to distance himself from politics, both those practiced by the Vietnamese and those back in the United States. He favored bombing North Vietnam, but only to gain military advantage. The general relied on body counts to tell whether his troops were successful. Unfortunately, people under his command became obsessed (and not always truthful) about the numbers of enemy bodies found following a battle.

But the Tet offensive of 1968 was the event that caused Westmoreland to leave Vietnam. Immediately after the offensive ended, Westmoreland asked for 206,000 more Americans. U.S. citizens were outraged. He was replaced in June, 1968, by General Creighton Abrams. When Westmoreland returned to the United States, he was named chief of staff of the army.

Long after the war, in 1982, a retired William Westmoreland sued CBS-TV, claiming that the network had unjustly accused him of lying. Reporters had indicated that Westmoreland falsified the number of enemy troops in Vietnam at the start of the Tet offensive. The general forced CBS to admit its reporting mistakes, and he did not press matters further.

Protests began in the United States, too. Young men by the thousands were drafted into the military in a system run by the Selective Service. This office of the federal government registered eighteen-year-olds and sent draft notices (orders to report for military service) to men aged nineteen or older. College students were not called up but were instead told they would be deferred; they would not be drafted until they had completed their studies. Nevertheless, students on the college campuses began to stage demonstrations against the draft and to harass military recruiters. Chants of "Hell no, we won't go," echoed across campuses large and small.

Small groups of radical students against the war were joined by many others who did not want their lives or educations disrupted. A popular wire service photo at the time showed college students burning their draft cards, the identification card every young American man was ordered to carry by the Selective Service. As more and more men were needed to fill military slots, the government lowered its standards. One basic-training unit at Fort Knox, Kentucky, in the fall of 1966, included a man who had only one lung and another who was let out of a Michigan prison in exchange for a promise to serve his country!

The Viet Cong were joined by more and more North Vietnamese regulars. These tough soldiers entered Vietnam by walking hundreds of miles down a concealed path known as the Ho Chi Minh Trail. The trail wound through forbidding jungle in Vietnam, Laos, and Cambodia. Despite bombing it day and night for years, the United States was unable to stop the trail's flow of soldiers and supplies. Weapons from Russia and China were delivered by train and boat into North Vietnam and then strapped to bicycles or slung over shoulders for the perilous trip south. Many North Vietnamese soldiers suffered from malaria or were injured or killed by American bombs.

The War and Its Weapons

Air strikes over North Vietnam intensified in 1965. U.S. pilots met a hail of antiaircraft fire, which was joined later in the war by surface-to-air missiles. The North Vietnamese had few aircraft, but every target of any importance in the north was ringed by antiaircraft weapons pointed toward the sky. U.S. planes were the best and U.S. pilots the most thoroughly trained. Nevertheless, many Americans were shot down over the north. Those who reached the ground alive were held in the "Hanoi Hilton" (the Hanoi City Jail) and smaller prisons. It would be years before they would be released. To this day, no accurate account of all American prisoners in Southeast Asia has taken place.

The marines sent in to protect the Danang air base, were joined by twenty-five thousand army, navy, and air force personnel who were told that they must "win the hearts and minds of the Vietnamese people." Young and frightened, American enlisted personnel forgot about goals and slogans and hoped to stay alive for their tour of duty — thirteen months for the marines and a year for all other service personnel.

A Vietnam-era American soldier was very well armed. In fact, an eight- or ten-man squad could produce as much firepower as a World

By 1967, the U.S. had loosed more bombs on Vietnam than the allies dropped during the whole of World War II. President Johnson relied increasingly on air power rather than ground combat because it cost fewer lives. Strategic Air Command B52s like these targeted Viet Cong roads, railways, factories, and homes. Each of the "Stratofortresses" was capable of carrying a conventional bomb load of up to 60,000 lbs.

War II platoon of thirty or more soldiers. The modern squad could include an M-60 machine gun, with one man carrying the gun and another carrying the belt of ammunition; one man carrying a grenade launcher that could fire grenade shells more than 100 yards and looked like a shotgun; four riflemen, each one equipped with an M-16 rifle that could fire as many as twenty bullets automatically; and perhaps one man with a shotgun. The squad could call in either air support or artillery via a mobile radio. Other squads might have had two men carrying the tube, base plate, and shells of a small piece of artillery called a mortar.

Viet Cong and North Vietnamese troops carried weapons from the Korean War, or newer arms from China or the Soviet Union. The backbone of the Communist arsenal was the AK-47, an automatic rifle considered by some to be superior to the American-made M-16 because the AK-47 continued to fire in water, sand, or mud. The M-16 operated flawlessly — if it was cleaned on a regular basis. Despite the many guns on each side, the most common injury was from shrapnel — tiny

the war and replaced Westmoreland with General Creighton Abrams. Clifford and others advised President Johnson against further expanding the war.

The earliest attacks on Johnson's Vietnam policy had come from those he understood least: young people, intellectuals, and certain members of the clergy. While these groups were greatly outnumbered by what would in 1968 be labeled by Richard Nixon the "Silent majority" of Americans, they had real influence on many Democratic members of the House of Representatives and the Senate. Working together, they staged a series of war protests that grew larger as the United States became more deeply involved in the war. Though peace demonstrations drew bigger crowds during the Nixon Administration that would follow, pacifists could easily rally as many as fifty thousand activists for rallies witnessed by LBJ in the nation's capital.

When Johnson ordered the bombing of North Vietnam in 1965, the antiwar movement had mushroomed. On April 17, twenty-thousand people converged on Washington for the SDS's first major antiwar rally. The SDS also helped organize university "teach-in," where students and professors gathered to discuss U.S. foreign policy, sing folk songs, and debate the war.

By 1967, the antiwar movement had widened. In February of that year, 2,500 mostly middle-class housewives from the Women Strike for Peace movement stormed the

Jane Fonda.

The daughter of actor Henry Fonda, Jane Fonda grew up in California and attended an exclusive college, Vassar, in New York State. Shortly afterward, she began to be featured in the movies. Several of the films, such as Barbarella, exploited her good looks. But no one denied that she could think or that she knew how to act.

By the mid-1960s, Fonda and a number of other celebrities were involved in antiwar activities. She did several things that bothered the Johnson and Nixon administrations. Aware that Bob Hope entertained troops in a prowar atmosphere, she formed a group of entertainers who went to Vietnam as part of an antiwar show tour. In 1972, she visited Hanoi to see for herself the damage created by U.S. bombing. Photographed wearing a North Vietnamese army helmet, it was suggested that she was being used for propaganda purposes by the North Vietnamese.

Fonda was divorced from Roger Vadim, a French movie mogul who made several of her earlier pictures. As the war wound down, she married Tom Hayden, a radical and one of the founders of the Students for a Democratic Society (SDS). Her marriage to Hayden did not last, but her career took off once hostilities in Southeast Asia ceased. She won Oscars and an Emmy for her dramatic performances in politically charged films, and she put together a series of exercise videotapes that are best-sellers today.

Her activism during the war still annoys some veterans and other members of the public. Asked today about the 1960s, Fonda says she was an antiwar activist because "I just wanted the killing to stop."

> *"What the hell is going on? I thought we were winning the war!... To say we are closer to victory today is to believe, in the face of the evidence, the optimists who have been wrong in the past."*
>
> Walter Cronkite, after visiting Saigon soon after Tet

> *"If I've lost Walter [Cronkite], then it's over. I've lost Mr. Average Citizen."*
>
> President Johnson

Pentagon, demanding to see the men who were sending their boys to war. Before the Tet offensive the hawks, those who were broadly behind the war, outnumbered the doves, those opposed to the war, 62 percent to 22 percent. Tet changed all that, shifting the balance to 41 percent hawks and 42 percent doves.

The media, too, was turning against the war and against the president. In June, 1960, South Vietnam's President Diem was described in Newsweek as "one of Asia's ablest leaders." By 1968, following Tet, James Reston, writing in the *New York Times*, would ask, "What is the end that justified this slaughter? How will we save Vietnam if we destroy it in the battle?"

Meanwhile, in Vietnam, troops learned that President Johnson had

"I Want Out" was an American antiwar poster parodying the Uncle Sam recruiting poster: "I Want You for the U.S. Army," which was popular during World War I.

ordered a bombing halt over the north, offered peace talks, and stated that he would not seek reelection. Despite Johnson's gestures for peace in the spring of 1968, the war continued. He remained the target of many antiwar demonstrations. Chants of "Hey, hey, LBJ, how many kids did you kill today?" were heard in the Oval Office as antiwar groups demonstrated in front of the White House. More and more fresh soldiers arriving for the one-year tour of duty in Vietnam told tales of antiwar fervor or defiant acts in the United States.

Many arrived as members of the counterculture, even though their shoulder-length hair was cut off and stayed off. They flew to Vietnam with African-American troops, some of whom had witnessed or joined in urban rioting, and were committed to Black Power. Other soldiers included Latinos and blue-collar whites. The military was careful not to place too many members of the same ethnic group in combat units, fearing that their orders would meet with an organized refusal. Vietnam was not a war between yellow men and white or black men, but was instead a war of peasants versus America's wealthy middle and lower-middle classes.

As the year ended, Richard Nixon won a close election for the presidency over Hubert Humphrey. Troop strength in Vietnam was 540,000 Americans.

Henry Kissinger, named a national security advisor by President Nixon, met in 1969 with North Vietnamese and Viet Cong representatives in Paris. The talks were aimed at stopping the war, but the conflict continued in new and horrible ways. The president ordered secret bombing of Vietnam's neighbor, Cambodia, in March. He did so because North Vietnamese troops were using Cambodia as a base, darting into South Vietnam on raids and then returning to safety in the supposedly neutral country. While this policy bothered many Americans, it faded from memory quickly in comparison to a year-old event that took place far to the north, near the demilitarized zone.

My Lai 4

On March 16, 1968, about 130 U.S. Army soldiers murdered between two hundred and six hundred children, women, and old people in a village called My Lai 4. The massacre did not become public knowledge until late 1969, when Ron Ridenhour, a helicopter door gunner, wrote numerous letters to U.S. senators and representatives. Ridenhour had seen some of the violence and it haunted him. But he had said little about it until he was discharged from the army for fear that he would be killed. Soldiers who had been at My Lai on that fateful day in 1968 quickly confirmed Ridenhour's "dark and bloody" story. . . .

Members of the American Division had lost a number of men to booby traps, tripped as the soldiers combed an area south of Danang for the enemy. These infantrymen, part of Charlie Company, were terribly unlucky. They had unknowingly entered a minefield created by Korean allies who had not told the Americans about the mines. Six members of the unit were killed and twelve injured. The men had seen no one but Vietnamese civilians and had assumed

Vietnam War

For further information see primary source entries on pages

12: 1638-43, 1660-63

the civilians were making booby traps for the Viet Cong and North Vietnamese.

Their leaders, Captain Ernest Medina and Lieutenant William L. Calley, Jr., tried to improve morale by telling the men they were going on an operation where the enemy would be numerous — in the village of My Lai 4. Medina and Calley led Company C into the village, where the Americans tossed hand grenades into huts, chased down and shot young and old, and killed animals with guns and bayonets. Lieutenant Calley herded about 100 civilians into a shallow ditch and, with several fellow soldiers, shot them to death with automatic rifles. The Americans then walked along the ditch, shooting anyone who moved.

More innocent lives might have been lost but for the bravery of a helicopter pilot, Hugh Thompson. Thompson saw the dead in the ditch and landed his craft, only to discover he was too late to save them. He returned to his helicopter and, seeing a group of women and children huddled nearby, flew his helicopter between the civilians and Calley's men. Thompson ordered his door gunner, armed with an M-60 machine gun, to shoot anyone who tried to harm the Vietnamese. The pilot landed the craft again, gathered the terrified Vietnamese, and flew out of the village.

A few soldiers in Company C did not take part in the massacre. One soldier shot himself in the foot so that he would not have to kill unarmed civilians. A reporter and a photographer took hundreds of color and black-and-white pictures of the bloodshed. Neither had much combat experience, but both believed they had seen a massacre. Eyewitnesses later said that at least 500 people lost their lives.

Captain Medina reported killing 128 Viet Cong. If that were true, how could only three weapons have been captured? How could the only American casualty have been one soldier's self-inflicted wound? Medina and Calley were arrested late in 1969 and charged with the deaths of more than 100 Vietnamese civilians. By March, 1970, a total of fourteen officers had been charged with covering up the massacre. On March 29, 1971, William Calley was found guilty of killing twenty-two civilians. His life term later was reduced to twenty years in prison. He was paroled in 1974. Calley was the only person who served any prison time in connection with the massacre.

Other terrible events related to the war took place in 1970. U.S. ground forces joined the South Vietnamese in an ill-conceived invasion of Cambodia that largely displaced or killed innocent civilians. Back home, members of the Ohio National Guard killed four antiwar demonstrators and wounded eleven on the campus of Kent State University in Ohio. Ohio governor James Rhodes had ordered the guardsmen on to the more usually apathetic campus after bottles were thrown at police during a protest against the U.S. invasion of Cambodia. The guardsmen opened fire on the unarmed students, claiming they had heard a shot.

But nothing approached the horror of the 1968 massacre in My Lai 4. The mother of a Company C soldier said, "I gave them a nice boy. They gave me back a murderer."

There seemed to be no one to admire in the war, though numerous

> *"There is no light at the end of the tunnel, only the darkness that came over my husband."*
>
> Judy Droz, war widow

brave men won the Medal of Honor by giving up their lives. A group of Green Berets was caught splashing Viet Cong flags with chicken blood and then selling the flags as souvenirs. A soldier in the army became so fed up with the paperwork for medals awarded to officers that he put through an order giving a medal to an officer's dog! By the end of 1970, the number of American soldiers in Vietnam was 280,000. The central question asked by many was, "Just why are we here anyway?"

This map shows the sites of major battles, bombing raids, and U.S. bases during the Vietnam War.

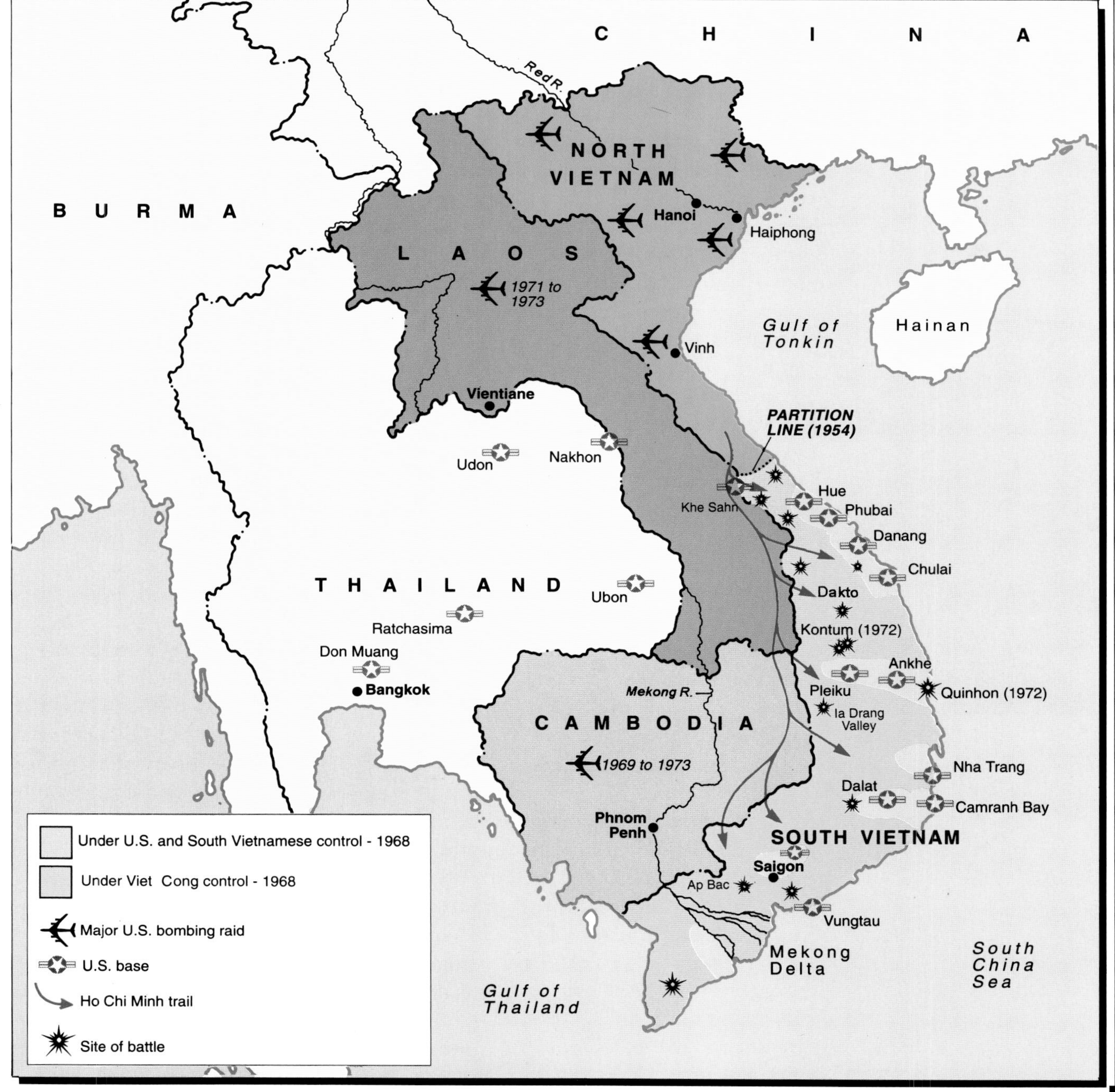

CHAPTER 8 Technology: Marvels and Limits

"Occasionally, I lie in bed at night and think now what in the hell do I want to get up on that thing?"

Virgil Grissom, astronaut

The 1960s was a decade of tremendous advances in all areas of science and technology. When the decade opened, manned spaceflight was still a dream; by the time of its close, astronauts had successfully landed on the moon. The race into space also brought us weather and telecommunications satellites, while lasers, robots, microchip computers and supersonic passenger travel began to revolutionize everyday life, bringing science fiction closer to reality. Meanwhile great advances were taking place in medicine, like the wider availability of vaccines and organ transplants, and a better understanding of the effects on health of diet and smoking.

The United States led the world in the field and Americans could be excused for believing that science and technology could help solve all of the world's problems.

The Space Race

The space race brought with it great technological advancements. Americans became the first and only human beings to reach the moon. That feat took place on July 20, 1969, when astronaut Neil A. Armstrong took a stroll on the lunar surface and said, "That's one small step for a man, one giant leap for mankind." His walk was witnessed by fellow astronaut Edwin E. "Buzz" Aldrin, Jr., and by people all across the globe as a live video camera transmitted the event directly to earth.

It seems incredible that the country could carry on a costly war, maintain new social programs, and pay for space probes, but the United States was a fairly incredible place during the decade.

Years of money, work, and sacrifice had gone into making the moon landing possible. The first American to achieve suborbital space flight was Alan B. Shepard, Jr. He rocketed 116 miles above the earth in 1961 in a Mercury capsule launched on a rocket from Cape Canaveral, Florida. The following year, John H. Glenn, Jr. became the first American to orbit the earth. He did so aboard a Mercury capsule called *Friendship* 7. It circled the globe three times before returning to earth.

Human progress in outer space came about because the United States and the Soviet Union were competing to see who could lead in such exploration. The Soviets launched their first unmanned satellite in 1957, and they followed that success with several other firsts. A month before Alan Shepard's flight, a Soviet by the name of Yuri A. Gagarin was fired into space and returned safely. The Soviets stayed ahead of American efforts for several years, becoming the first to launch their cosmonauts into space in a container that made space suits unnecessary. The first person to "walk" in space by leaving a capsule and floating on a line was Soviet Aleksei A. Leonov. He performed a ten-minute walk in 1965.

Occasionally, there were grim reminders that human life was involved and could be destroyed. Leonid Brezhnev, Soviet premier from 1964 to 1982, talked tearfully to cosmonaut Vladimir Komarov on April 23, 1967, while Komarov's *Soyuz I* spacecraft burned up on re-entering earth's atmosphere. Earlier the same year, three U.S. astronauts had burned to death in a fire that swept their *Apollo I* craft. Roger B.

First men on the moon, July 20, 1969. Neil Armstrong and the lunar module are reflected in Buzz Aldrin's visor. Although most Americans considered this one of the nation's greatest achievements, the black leader Rev. Jesse Jackson commented: "How can this nation swell and swagger with technological pride when it has a spiritual will so crippled."

SPACE

For further information see primary source entries on pages

12: 1625-26, 1694-96

Chaffee, Virgil I. Grissom, and Edward H. White died on January 27 in the space capsule on the ground at Cape Kennedy in Florida.

During the sixties, both the United States and the Soviet Union successfully put into orbit numerous unmanned satellites that helped them do everything from predict the weather to spy on each other. Despite continued mistrust, Soviets and Americans would go on to stage joint space operations. But nothing could eclipse the three moon landings made by American astronauts between 1969 and 1971.

The revolutionary new communications satellite, Telstar, *was sent into orbit on July 11, 1962, marking the beginning of transatlantic TV transmission.*

Americans today take for granted many of the niceties created by various probes into space. Rural residents with satellite dishes now receive dozens of television channels beamed from television stations to an orbiting satellite and back to receiving dishes everywhere. Live television in Iran, Somalia, and elsewhere is made possible with that same satellite technology. Transoceanic telephone calls and facsimile messages can be sent immediately into space, and just as quickly routed to England, Singapore, or Rio de Janiero. Other technical benefits of the space program range from the miniaturization of communications devices and better solar-powered batteries, to the creation of new plant hybrids, dehydrated foods, and the manufacture of medicines in weightless conditions.

War Technology

Throughout history, war has been a great spur to technological improvement. This was true during World War I, when airplanes and tanks were first developed for use in conflict. During World War II, it was the atomic bomb and missile technology that took a leap forward.

During the war in Vietnam, many new and horrific weapons were developed to cope with the unusual fighting situations in which the U.S. troops found themselves. The Viet Cong could hide out in the dense foliage of the rainforest, so powerful defoliants were developed. American planes flew over the knotted vegetation, spraying liquids that withered leaves and dried up growing plants. Unfortunately, at least one such herbicide, Agent Orange, may have had lasting effects on human beings. Returning U.S. soldiers complained about rashes, about cancer they suffered or cancer in their newborn children, about blinding headaches, and about other aches and pains that did not respond to treatment. Many veterans were convinced that Agent Orange was the source of their problems, though they had no proof.

Napalm, by the latter part of the 1960s, was as familiar to Americans as tires or antifreeze or anything else seen regularly on network television. The high-tech bombs of jellied gasoline were shown frequently on the evening news, tumbling from the bellies of U.S. and South Vietnamese planes to create a horrifying wave of liquid fire that killed or maimed everything in its path. One of the most famous wire-service photos from the war shows a preteen Vietnamese girl, her clothing burned off by napalm, running in pain and terror down a village road toward the photographer.

Produced by the Dow Chemical Company in Michigan, napalm was just one of many advanced weapons used in Vietnam. There were others, among them an artillery shell filled with small metal darts, or *flechettes*. On impact, the shell blew apart, sending darts buzzing like a high-speed swarm of bees in all directions. U.S. Army Ninth Infantry Division soldiers once found a dead enemy soldier standing pinned to a tree by hundreds of the darts. Other shells produced substances such as molten white phosphorus which burnt on contact.

Several weapons used against human beings had been outlawed for years by the Geneva convention on warfare — but they were used anyway. For example, fifty-caliber machine guns with bullets the size of railroad spikes were fired illegally at ground troops.

There were many other high-tech creations. U.S. forces had night scopes that allowed them to look through special lenses and see movement in the dark. They also had LAWs, light anti-tank weapons. Such one-person devices featured a sight on a fiberglass barrel that was disposed of once the single shell was fired. The shell was designed to penetrate tank armor but was just as effective when used on fortified enemy positions.

High above the ground, air force and navy pilots and crews used many other technological marvels. A pilot

Over 12 million gallons of chemical herbicide code-named Agent Orange were sprayed over the mangrove forests of Vietnam causing long-term ecological damage. The top photo, is an aerial view of an unsprayed forest 60 miles from Saigon. Below, is a nearby forest sprayed with the defoliant sometime before 1968.

The air force fighter F-111A was introduced during the Vietnam war in 1966. It was specially designed for low level attack and proved extremely successful in finding its target whatever the weather conditions.

flying over North Vietnam learned instantly if radar, used by the North Vietnamese to target their ground-to-air missiles, was aimed at his craft. He could then take evasive action or fire an air-to-ground missile that would follow the invisible radar beam back to its source! One advanced U.S. jet flew so quietly and so low toward targets that radar could not track it. This plane featured a computer that adjusted the plane's altitude to the changing surface of the earth below. Other, slower, propeller-driven planes tracked movements of vehicles and troops at night with equipment that sensed heat from engines or from human bodies.

Modern Medicines

The most noteworthy medical news of the 1960s by far involved the human heart. A South African surgeon, Christiaan Barnard, led a twenty-person team in 1967 in successfully removing the diseased heart of Louis Washkansky, an incurably ill South African grocer, and replacing it with the heart of an accident victim. Although the transplant itself was successful, Washkansky died eighteen days later from double pneumonia he contracted after the drugs given him to prevent rejection of the new heart, had unfortunately destroyed his body's immune system.

Barnard, who studied at the University of Minnesota, also introduced open-heart surgery to South Africa and developed a new design for artificial heart valves, which were often used in open-heart work. It was no accident that Dr. Barnard studied at Minnesota. The medical school there included a surgeon named Floyd John Lewis. He introduced hypothermia — lowering the patient's body temperature so the heart would stop beating during open-heart operations.

Other organs had been transplanted earlier. Lungs and livers were transplanted in separate operations in 1963. A pancreas had been first transplanted in 1966. Kidney transplants were more than fifty years old by the 1960s, though the operation became successful only after work in Boston in 1954 took it beyond the experimental stage.

During the decade, vaccines were introduced that prevented measles and rubella (German measles). The latter was especially important for women, who could pass deformities on to the child they were carrying if they contracted the disease during pregnancy. By 1960, polio could be prevented with an oral dose rather than an injection. The decade saw progress against cancer, too. Surgery was the usual therapy, but radiation and chemotherapy played increasingly important roles. Better understanding of the body's endocrine glands meant that, among other things, couples could more easily be treated for infertility. Ironically, the 1960s were also the decade when the birth control pill came into widespread use worldwide. For the first time in history, women could control family size, and when and whether their bodies would bear children.

American families in the early sixties were saved from a terrible medical mishap by the diligence of a strong-willed woman and a government agency. Dr. Frances Oldham Kelsey, a pharmacologist with the Food and Drug Administration (FDA), refused to allow a European drug company to sell sleeping pills called thalidomide in the United States. Dr. Kelsey insisted that not enough tests had been conducted to prove the safety of the pills. The doctor was proven correct a year later, when ten thousand deformed babies with damaged organs and dwarfed arms and legs were born to European mothers who had taken thalidomide during pregnancy. The pharmacologist's adherence to high standards won for her the Presidential Award for Distinguished Service in 1963.

Cancer came under intense scrutiny in the sixties. Despite public pressure, the FDA refused to approve any of several "miracle" cures for cancer. The most widely known, Krebiozen, they termed worthless. Those who sought it anyhow had to go to Mexico for a dose of the substance. At about the same time, the federal Public Health Service issued a report branding cigarettes a leading cause of cancer, heart disease, and other fatal illnesses. Tobacco companies were forced to stop advertising on television and were ordered by Congress to carry warning labels on their packs and in print advertising indicating that they were harmful.

Pharmaceutical specialist Dr. Frances Kelsey, pictured with her daughters Christine and Susan, is said to have prevented an American tragedy by refusing to allow the drug thalidomide to be marketed in the U.S. Later, thousands of European babies were born with horrific physical deformities as a result of their mothers taking the sleeping pill during pregnancy.

American advertisement for Kent cigarettes in 1964. After the Surgeon General had announced that cigarette smoking was the main cause of lung cancer and bronchitis, as well as being a contributory factor to heart disease, ulcers, and other ailments, tobacco companies were compelled to print warnings on all their ads and on the cigarette packs.

Healthy Food

Meanwhile, in many homes across the country, people began to examine more closely exactly what they were eating. A health-food craze that began in California spread across the land, bringing with it granola, wheat germ and wheat bran, servings of fruits and vegetables with each meal, and even organically grown (pesticide-free) foods. As adults accepted the newer foods, they began to question the traditional diet of cheeseburgers, french-fried potatoes, and milkshakes, all of which dripped with animal fat. Doctors and nurses who performed heart-bypass surgery told of veins and arteries clogged with a sticky substance called cholesterol that was traced to excessive eating of animal fat. Burgers, fries, shakes, sundaes, chips, and desserts came to be called "junk food." So did soft drinks, candy, and other snacks that furnished sugar and energy but little nutrition.

Guidance Counseling

With everyone looking out for the body's welfare, who was looking out for the mind? The practice of psychiatry and psychology boomed as humans became more confident about attacking and overcoming depression, neurosis, psychosis, and other mental disturbances. A new kind of professional appeared in public schools, called a guidance counselor. Such professionals helped students select the right training, jobs, and colleges after high school. These people often held master's degrees in psychology or in counseling, and even worked with law enforcement in matters of juvenile delinquency, alcohol and drug use, and child abuse. By the decade's end, many had steered young men away from the military by finding colleges for them to attend. The war in Vietnam had a lot to do with the sixties' boom in college enrollment.

The Laser

Affecting medicine and much else was a new kind of light called the laser. Lasers are intense beams of a single, very pure color. Laser is an acronym for Light Amplification by Stimulated Emission of Radiation. The first gas-discharge laser was constructed by three Bell Laboratories scientists in New Jersey in 1960. Its use is widespread and growing today.

There are all kinds of lasers, produced by chemicals, optical equipment, gases, special dyes, and more. Some laser wavelengths can be tuned, or controlled. These are the most useful to science, which uses them as precise scalpels in eye and other surgery or for exact measurements. Laser beams have measured the distance between the earth and the moon more exactly than has any other device. No single laser is suitable for all purposes, but some lasers can do things thought impossible before they were developed.

Farming and Modern Technologies

In rural America, there were also changes in the business of agriculture. Fewer and fewer farmers and farm workers were producing bigger and bigger crops, thanks to better seed, fertilizer, chemicals, and farming tools. Domesticated animals such as cattle, pigs, sheep, and chickens were producing healthier offspring, because scientists were exploring how animals pass on characteristics to their offspring. The leanest, healthiest animals were mated by artificial insemination. Farm workers waited until a female came into heat, then impregnated her with sperm extracted from a male that may have been several states away. The results were calves, piglets, lambs, and chicks that could be guaranteed to produce more food.

Americans may be excused for believing that, with improving agricultural science and technology, farmers could at last assert full control over the land they worked. Chemicals could be used to control pests, increase fertility of the land, and raise productivity. There seemed no limit to what science could achieve. In 1962, however, that smug illusion was shattered.

"Silent Spring"

The thin, timid, scholarly woman moved closer to the microphone so the politicians could hear. Yes, she assured the members of Congress, she was a longtime government employee trained in biology, not a writer seeking attention. Her name was Rachel Carson, and she told the politicians of the terrible long-term effects of chemical herbicides and pesticides on the environment. Carson reported that DDT, used by farmers nationwide to keep pests off fruits and vegetables, was slowly poisoning the earth. Her award-winning book, *Silent Spring*, repeated the scientist's testimony by portraying an earth where no birds sang, crickets chirped, or dogs barked — all had been slowly poisoned.

ENVIRONMENT

For further information see primary source entries on pages

11: 1471-73; **12:** 1663-65, 1669-71, 1711-13

An intense ruby laser light beam penetrates two prisms during an experiment designed to improve laser devices at the Autonetics Division of North American Aviation in California, 1965. The first gas-discharge laser was created in New Jersey in 1960.

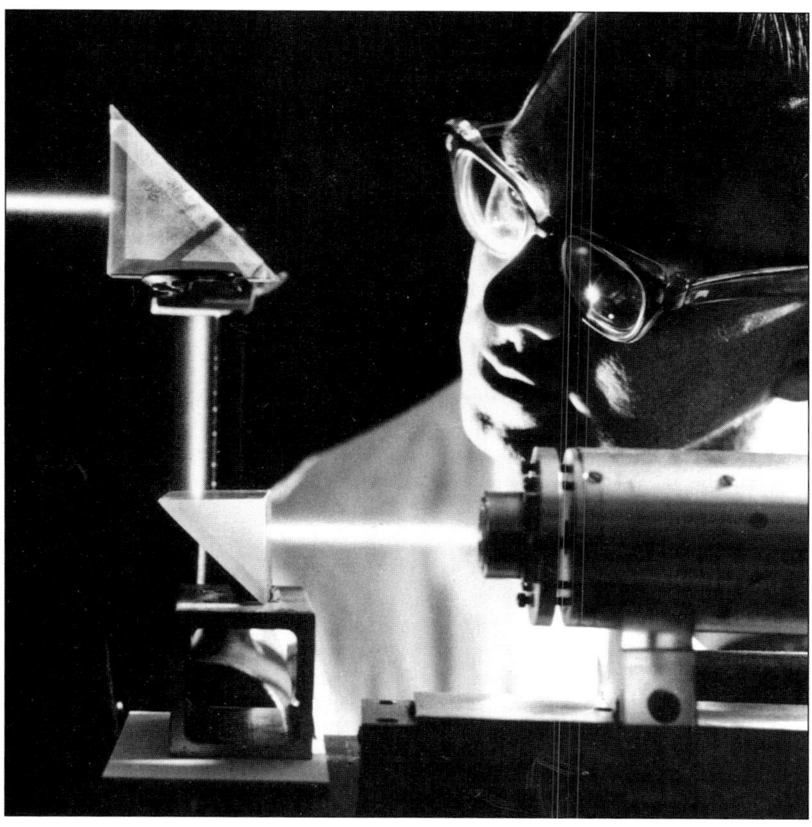

Rachel Carson. (1907-1964)

The "nun of nature," Rachel Carson, was a quiet, shy person who had an almost religious feeling about the environment. Born in a rural valley in Pennsylvania, she was a smart and observant child who watched what went on in the natural world.

She entered Pennsylvania College for Women, learning to write well as she studied zoology. Graduating with high honors in 1928, she went on to study zoology and genetics at Johns Hopkins University in Baltimore, graduating just as the Great Depression began.

Carson taught at Johns Hopkins and at the University of Maryland. Summers were spent at the Woods Hole biological laboratory in Massachusetts. All the while, she submitted prose and verse to major magazines, collecting many rejection slips but getting better with each effort. She moved to Washington, D.C., in 1936 to become a writer for the federal Bureau of Fisheries.

Her first major essay, entitled *Undersea,* was purchased shortly afterward by *Atlantic* magazine. A nonfiction book, *Under the Sea-Wind*, followed, but its importance was overshadowed by the start of World War II. Yet several authorities noticed the power of her prose, which appeared later in other books. But nothing prepared either Carson or her readers for the popularity of *Silent Spring*, which came out in 1962.

For years, she had noticed the deaths of aquatic life in swamps and along seashores, the results of contact with pesticides. Carson knew that farmers killed weeds, bugs, and microscopic organisms in order to grow bigger and better crops. But did those farmers know what Carson observed — that birds eating pesticide-covered bugs passed the deadly chemicals on to their offspring? Worse, did farmers realize that the weedkiller sprayed on feeds traveled through their cattle and on to dining-room tables?

Carson used a devastating technique to make her point. *Silent Spring* begins by telling of a world where no birds sing, no plants flower, and no fish swim. It is dead because human beings killed it with too much pesticide. The book began to sell and has never stopped. More important, *Silent Spring* became the Bible of the modern environmental movement.

Carson testified before Congress, confirming her words with stark names, numbers, and lists of species that pesticides had made extinct. Chemical companies attacked her viciously, but the worst thing anyone could say about the biologist and writer was that she preferred the company of nature to that of human beings.

DDT, a popular pesticide, was labeled by Carson and others as a cause of cancer. The power of her book caused production of the deadly chemical to cease. Companies such as Velsicol threatened to sue, and Monsanto had its employees write a book-length answer to *Silent Spring*. Carson's work was backed by John F. Kennedy's Science Advisory Committee, and only the most foolish chemical companies continued to complain as she campaigned to get such poisons banned.

By 1963, *Silent Spring* had been published in more than a dozen languages, was endorsed by Britain's Prince Philip, and featured on a CBS-TV special, "The Silent Spring of Rachel Carson." Sadly, she was unable to enjoy much of the continuing applause — Rachel Carson was afflicted with cancer. She died on April 14, 1964, at the age of fifty-six. Carson is important for her writing, which changed the way we live, and as a role model to women and men dedicated to the environment who would follow.

It is no exaggeration to say that Rachel Carson's low-key testimony and her moving book started the modern environmental movement. Before Rachel Carson testified that pesticides were being passed from mother to child in breast milk, groups such as the Sierra Club and the Audubon Society were looked on as dizzy but likeable fresh-air freaks. DDT was quickly banned, and chemical companies were forced to develop less dangerous substitutes by regulation. Carson, who died of cancer in 1964, won the National Book Award in 1962 for *Silent Spring*.

If the food we ate was potentially harmful, what else was dangerous? Even before *Silent Spring*, government officials were aware that streams, rivers, lakes, and oceans were being fouled. In at least fifteen hundred communities, sewage and industrial wastes had been dumped into the same sources used for drinking water. Because states and communities were not sufficiently controlling pollution, Congress passed, in 1961, the Water Pollution Control Act. Although few polluters were prosecuted during the 1960s, many were forced to clean up their acts.

This aerial view of Manhattan in 1967 shows an enveloping smog just after a Public Health Service report that New York had the worst air pollution problem of any major metropolitan area in the nation.

Cleaner Air, Safer Cars

The smog hanging over Los Angeles had first been noticed during World War II, but the first hints of widespread air pollution came from commercial airline pilots, who reported thin layers of murky, brown air over places such as Denver and Phoenix. As so often is the case, however, it took a tragedy for something to be done. On Thanksgiving Day 1966, stagnant air trapped by unusual weather killed 168 elderly persons and people with respiratory problems in New York City. A federal Clean Air Act had been passed in 1963, but it had merely increased financial and technical assistance to state and local pollution-control agencies. Following the New York City mishap and constant reports of foul air from cars in the Los Angeles basin, a 1967 federal act set standards for the kinds of materials that could be legally puffed out of smokestacks.

If Rachel Carson is the mother of modern environmentalism, Ralph Nader is the father of contemporary car safety. A brilliant and incorruptible lawyer, Nader's book, *Unsafe at Any Speed*, was published in 1965. The work told of the many dangers to passengers in cars produced by America's major automakers. Nader's pressure led to the creation of the Vehicle Safety Act in 1966. Regulations were written concerning interior padding and headrests, safety belts, and glass that crumbled to a "gravel" rather than shattering into death-dealing shards.

Ralph Nader obtained financing for additional good works in an unusual way. General Motors had hired a private detective to shadow the attorney. They reasoned that there was something in his background they could use to silence him. But Nader found out about the detective and successfully sued the carmaker. The $500,000 he received was poured back into issues that related to public safety. Nader ended the sixties with a flourish; in 1968, he exposed the dangers of pipelines that led to the Natural Gas Pipelines Act, and he told of fears about nuclear energy that resulted in the Radiation Control Act that same year.

The late 1960s saw the launch of the consumer movement. Perhaps it was created by the long-term artificially healthy economy. Many manufacturers had, until then, mass produced retail goods, not always paying attention to the quality of clothing, appliances, furniture, linens other items. Sears Roebuck and Co., with its slogan of "Satisfaction guaranteed or your money back," gained a whole new generation of shoppers. By 1970, there were seventeen million American families with a Sears credit card. Suddenly retailers and manufacturers that wanted to argue over returned goods found themselves doing less business.

It seems that, on the retail front, there were two paths to success: either offer something completely new or offer the same old thing in a new way. McDonald's restaurants chose the latter route, with tasty, inexpensive food served quickly. Customers stood at counters and waited for meals from the grill, from the deep fryer, or out of the soft-drink machine. McDonald's first chain restaurant, copied from a drive-in in California, was built in 1955 in Des Plaines, Illinois. Soon, they were

Ralph Nader.

Ralph Nader, "The Consumer Crusader," is the kind of person who emerged in the 1960s and has been seen too seldom since. He cared little for money, power, or fame, devoting himself instead to the good of the majority.

Nader, the son of Lebanese immigrants, grew up in Connecticut and graduated with honors from Princeton University. He also was an honors graduate of Harvard University, where he attended law school. An activist very early, he led an unsuccessful but stubborn campaign to prevent campus trees from being sprayed with the pesticide DDT. It was while at Harvard that he became interested in auto safety.

The link between the law and highway deaths was a strong one. Nader believed that drivers were blamed too often for accidents when in reality their cars failed them. The young lawyer went to Washington and worked with Connecticut Senator Abraham Ribicoff to reduce the "fantastic carnage" on American roads.

His book, *Unsafe at Any Speed: The Designed-in Dangers of the American Automobile*, came out in 1965. It pointed to dangers in many cars but concentrated on the Chevrolet Corvair, "one of the nastiest-handling cars ever built," Nader believed. The book was so important that Lyndon Johnson noted it in his 1966 State of the Union address, and it affected highway-safety legislation for years.

General Motors, maker of the Corvair, hired a detective to find out anything he could about Nader. But Ralph lived in a small and almost bare apartment, had no television set, stayed up late only to read and to write, and was incorruptible. He found out he was being shadowed, and he sued the automaker. The money he eventually won allowed him to set up several consumer organizations that eventually investigated other areas, such as the safety of interstate gas pipelines and attempts by the Reagan administration to label "top secret" anything it did not want the public to know.

Nader has written numerous books, most of them warning of dangers, scams, or illegal or unethical practices. Asked by Robert F. Kennedy why he was so involved, Nader answered, "If I were engaged in activities [against] cruelty to animals, nobody would ask me that question."

He remains active in the Public Interest Research Group and other Nader-conceived, nonprofit offices dedicated to protecting the public from government, big business, and other potentially harmful agencies. Nader's 1960s activism has never waned.

Ralph Nader speaks with veteran muckraking author, Upton Sinclair, at the White House after the signing of the Meat Inspection Bill, 1967.

everywhere. Imitators sprang up, too, wherever there was a busy intersection or a shopping area. Franchise owners usually realized handsome profits from their investment, while the next generation of American workers labored after school and on weekends under bright lights, behind Formica counters.

Quality and the Japanese

Throughout the sixties, more and better Japanese-made products found their way into American homes. It hardly happened overnight, since shoddy, short-lived trinkets from Japan had begun showing up shortly after World War II. But with each wave of imitations, the products became better. Motorcycles provide a good illustration of how the Japanese came to dominate a market.

Motorcycling in the United States once had a bad reputation. That reputation originated in a 1950s movie, *The Wild One*, starring Marlon Brando as a cycle-riding thug. Nevertheless, Honda introduced a tiny, 50cc two-wheeler about the time the first baby boomers were in high school. Radio ads featured Beach-Boys-type music and told consumers, "You meet the nicest people on a Honda." Thousands of the little bikes, with top speeds of about thirty-five miles an hour, were sold and proved to be top quality and lots of fun. When cycling baby boomers were ready for more speed, so were the Japanese.

The Japanese managed to capture a sizeable slice of the American motor cycle market with their Suzuki 80cc in 1964, since it cost less than any American-made equivalent.

Honda, Kawasaki, Suzuki, and Yamaha brought out motorcycles that were great to look at, fast, and cost much less than the only remaining American motorcycle, Harley-Davidson, or bikes imported from Europe. Japanese machines offered good gas mileage, simple maintenance, reliability, and a cheap way to see the country. Kids who never thought twice about the Hell's Angels pulled on helmets and roared off to school, jobs, and adventures. The *Wall Street Journal* called motorcycling a "boomlet." By the end of the sixties, there were ten million motorcycles on American roads. Everybody had a nephew, a brother, a father, or at least a friend who rode a motorcycle. Not widely seen as transportation, most were weekend toys.

Japanese motorcycles were joined by Datsun and Toyota cars, Canon and Minolta cameras, Mitsubishi and Sony TV sets, Akai and Teac tape recorders, and more. Because tastes differ from one country to the next, the cars sometimes took a little getting used to — a Japanese dealership might have a few lavender cars with light green interiors. To meet American preferences, Japanese automakers opened design studios in California and hired Americans to dream up new styles. Datsun brought out a sharp sports car in the late 1960s and was advised by its dealers not to call it by its Japanese model name, "Fair Lady." That car was introduced in America as the 240-Z, and it became one of the most popular sports cars ever built.

Inventions and improvements on existing products just kept coming. Smaller and smaller computers were able to do more and more jobs that once required hundreds of workers. From one end of the sixties, when a company called Digital introduced the minicomputer, to the other, when many firms kept track of vast quantities of information with a keyboard and small screen, the future had arrived.

CHAPTER 9
The Medium Is the Message

"The biggest mistake in my political life was not to learn how to use television."

So said Hubert H. Humphrey after narrowly losing the 1968 presidential election to Richard M. Nixon. His remark is surprising, since TV had already played a significant role in both the 1960 and 1964 presidential races.

Televising the Candidates

Millions of Americans gathered around their black and white television sets in the fall of 1960 to watch the first of four pre-election debates between Republican candidate Nixon and Democratic candidate John F. Kennedy. Kennedy, who looked calm and more sure of himself before the cameras, went on to edge out the former vice president in one of the closest national elections in history.

If Humphrey needed proof of the power of TV in 1968, all he needed to do was recall the 1964 election. Democrats Lyndon B. Johnson and Humphrey himself were running against Barry Goldwater and William Miller for president and vice president, respectively. Johnson portrayed himself as the candidate of peace, and he did so in one crude but effective way. His most famous commercial showed a little girl happily counting the number of petals on a flower. As the camera closed in on her, her counting became the countdown for a missile. There followed the flash of an exploding atomic bomb. The commercial ran only once, but it became a classic. LBJ hinted repeatedly that Goldwater — a pilot in the Air Force Reserves, a conservative, and a friend of the military — might start World War III. Apparently, most voters believed the same thing.

By 1968, prominent Republican Party leaders had hired advertising experts to "package and sell" Richard Nixon to the American people. The candidate was always carefully made up and closely shaved. He was placed among people who would ask only approved questions on a stage or set that looked presidential. Although Humphrey made a single, effective television ad, it could not compete. Future political candidates would study Nixon's advertising to see how television could seal an election victory. A book by Joe McGinnis about the 1968 campaign showed Richard Nixon on a pack of cigarettes. The book was called *The Selling of the President*.

If television was enjoyable in black and white, it was positively addictive in color. Stations began broadcasting in color sometime in the mid-sixties, and color TVs became a popular purchase by the late sixties. Professional football was regular entertainment throughout the 1950s, but it came alive on Sunday afternoons in the 1960s when fans could munch chips, drink beer, and see the green and silver wings on the

> *"I invite you to sit down in front of your television sets...and stay there. You will see a vast wasteland — a procession of game shows, formula comedies about totally unbelievable families...blood and thunder...mayhem, violence, sadism, murder...and, endlessly, commercials — many screaming, cajoling and offending."*
>
> FCC chairman, Newton N. Minow, 1961

Philadelphia Eagles' helmets or the golden numerals on the royal blue jerseys of the Los Angeles Rams. There were only a dozen National Football League teams at the time, but they were joined in 1960 by the upstart American Football League. Both leagues prospered due to television, which helped create the football playoff known as the Super Bowl. The first Super Bowl, or title game between leagues, was played in 1967. The two leagues merged in 1970.

The Green Bay Packers, coached by Vince Lombardi, beat the Kansas City Chiefs 35-10 in the 1967 Super Bowl, then defeated the Oakland Raiders in the 1968 Super Bowl, 33-14. Fans assumed the NFL team would defeat the AFL representative in 1969, too, before a smooth-talking, gimpy-legged quarterback, Joe

The 1967 Super Bowl play-off between the Green Bay Packers and the Kansas City Chiefs.

Roger Maris. (1934-1985)

When the old-timers talk about major-league baseball, Roger Maris is the kind of player they remember. Maris was born in Hibbing, Minnesota, and grew up in Fargo, North Dakota. As a boy, he ran the 100-yard dash in ten seconds, earned all-state honors in football, and played Little League and city-league baseball.

After high school, Maris was offered a football scholarship to the University of Oklahoma. Instead, he joined a baseball team that was part of the Cleveland Indians' minor-league system. "I guess I wasn't smart enough to go to college," he said.

Standing six feet tall and weighing almost two hundred pounds, Maris was so strong and big through the shoulders that he was only comfortable in custom-made clothing. He could hit a baseball as far as anyone, he threw the ball with ease from the deepest spot in the outfield to home plate, and he sped around the bases. Despite his physical abilities, his career was plagued by mysterious batting slumps.

The powerful right fielder played his first major-league season in 1957 with the Cleveland Indians. After batting only .235 and getting a reputation as a sulker, Maris was traded in 1958 to Kansas City. The following year began with a bang as Roger averaged .328 early in the season. But he was stricken with appendicitis that required surgery, and he finished the year batting .273. That December, he was traded to the New York Yankees.

Maris joined Mickey Mantle to become the most threatening home-run duo since Babe Ruth and Lou Gehrig. Maris swung a bat so well in 1960 that he was named the American League's Most Valuable Player. By the middle of the 1961 season, fans came to the ball park just to see Maris or Mantle hit towering home runs. Maris hit sixty-one homers in 1961, breaking a record set by Babe Ruth thirty-four years earlier. Once again, Most Valuable Player honors went to Maris. No wonder Yankees manager Casey Stengel considered Maris "the best trade I ever made."

But Mantle was faster, got on base more often, and was less prone to batting slumps. Perhaps that is why he is in the Baseball Hall of Fame and Maris is not. Maris's final season in the major leagues was 1968.

Maris married his high-school sweetheart. They had a girl and three boys and settled down in a Kansas City suburb. Maris had few interests except baseball. He played an average game of golf but said he was too high-strung to read a book or write a letter.

For several big-league seasons in the 1960s, every kid in the western hemisphere who could swing a bat wanted to be Roger Maris. The man with the blond crewcut, big shoulders and home-run record died on December 14, 1985.

Namath of the New York Jets, prophesied, "I guarantee a victory" over the Baltimore Colts. The AFL Jets did indeed beat Baltimore, 16-7. Kansas City upheld AFL honors in 1970, beating the Minnesota Vikings by 23-7.

While baseball continued to be called America's pastime, professional football mushroomed in popularity in the 1960s, thanks primarily to the fact that almost every American home had a TV set. Football televised well, and the networks and teams adjusted the rules to enhance televised coverage. The immense popularity of professional basketball was several years away, as an increasing number of African-Americans showed how the game should be played. For several years, professional athletes had been increasingly easy to recognize as they appeared more and more close up on television rather than just in the grainy photos seen in daily newspapers. One result was that athletes made more money as advertisers sought them to endorse everything from panty hose to antiperspirant.

The decade's most famous athlete didn't receive many offers to endorse products. Nevertheless, Muhammad Ali was known all over the world. The Louisville native began boxing as Cassius Clay, changing his name when he accepted the religion of

"Nothin' but a fool would want to fight me. No one can beat me. I'm too fast."

Muhammad Ali

Muhammad Ali.

Muhammad Ali began life in Louisville, Kentucky, as Cassius Clay. He grew up tall, strong, and fast, becoming a boxer. Clay represented the United States in the 1960 Olympics, winning a gold medal in the light heavyweight division at the age of eighteen. By 1964, he was the world heavyweight champion, having defeated Sonny Liston.

Those are the facts, but facts alone don't do justice to Ali, who was one of the most entertaining sports personalities this country has ever produced. He boldly predicted victory after victory as heavyweight champ, almost always making good on his promises to "float like a butterfly and sting like a bee" as his slower opponents took a heavy drubbing.

Ali, as he came to be known after becoming a Black Muslim, was among the first widely known Americans to resist the Vietnam-era draft. As a minister in his faith and as a conscientious objector, he claimed he should be exempt from the military. When the government took him anyway, he refused induction. Ali appealed the sentence of five years in jail and the $10,000 fine. The World Boxing Association took Ali's title in 1967, and for the next several years Muhammad fought only the conviction.

He won the case against the government and then took back the heavyweight belt in 1974, beating George Foreman. For the next four years, Ali was his old self again. He mugged for the cameras, barked poetry into microphones, and moved around the boxing ring at a pace his opponents could not match. In 1975, he wrote an autobiography which was entitled *The Greatest, My Own Story.*

He retired from the ring for the final time in 1979, having won the crown a total of three times. But he could not stay away, returning in 1980 in a vain attempt to beat Larry Holmes. The many matches eventually took their toll — Ali today is slowed by Parkinson's Disease, barely able to move or talk.

Islam. In 1964, Clay knocked out Sonny Liston to capture the world heavyweight boxing crown. He held it until 1967, when it was taken away because Ali refused induction into the military, citing his religious beliefs. Many Americans turned on him, wondering how the boxer could pound someone senseless in the ring but not shoot an enemy with a rifle.

Ali was prosecuted for his failure to report for military duty. He won the right not to serve after several years of court battles. Remarkably, he regained the title in 1974. Sometimes abrasive, sometimes moody, sometimes a put-on artist, Ali posed for a magazine cover at the height of his draft troubles tied up and suffering from the wounds of several arrows! Throughout his marriages and in fights that took place everywhere from Africa to the Philippines, Ali was above all an entertainer.

Television, too, tried to keep you entertained no matter who or what you liked. Before moving to the West Coast, Dick Clark brought "American Bandstand" into American living rooms from Philadelphia each weekday afternoon. Kids from coast to coast in the 1960s tuned in after school to watch people their age dance to rock and roll music. Clark, who continues to be seen today on television, let his young guests rate new records and provided a national program where singers would pantomime their hits.

Top-rated TV Shows

Four of the most popular television shows of all time were broadcast during these ten years. The decade's most popular single show was part of the series known as "The Fugitive." Actor David Jansen portrayed a man whose wife had been killed and who was running from the law because he

David Jansen starred in the popular TV show The Fugitive *from 1963 to 1967; it sometimes drew over 50 percent ratings during its successful run.*

had been unjustly accused of her murder. As the hero dodged police and informants, he searched for a one-armed man whom he had seen at his home at the time of the killing. More than twenty-five million households tuned in to the final September 29, 1967, episode of "The Fuge."

Two 1964 programs were the second and third most popular shows of the decade. On February 9, 1964, before a live audience made up mostly of screaming teenage girls, "The Ed Sullivan Show" introduced The Beatles to America. Sullivan, an awkward New Yorker who wrote a newspaper column before serving as a television master of ceremonies, introduced many performers to a national audience, from Elvis Presley in the 1950s to The Rolling Stones,

The Who, and The Animals a short while after The Beatles.

The third most popular show was the network comedy, "The Beverly Hillbillies." This thirty-minute, weekly show had a clever premise: a family of West Virginians struck oil on their property and moved west into a mansion in a neighborhood full of celebrities. The unsophisticated former West Virginians got the best of a bunch of slick salespeople and flim-flam artists in at least one hundred different ways.

CBS offered thirteen of the fifteen most popular regularly scheduled shows during the 1960s. "The Red Skelton Show," "The Andy Griffith Show," "The Beverly Hillbillies," "The Ed Sullivan Show," "The Lucy Show," "The Jackie Gleason Show," "Gomer Pyle," "Candid Camera," "The Dick Van Dyke Show," "The Danny Thomas Show," "Family Affair," and "Rawhide" all were presented by CBS. NBC shows included "Bonanza" and "Laugh-In," while ABC-TV scored with "Bewitched." Shows popular with teenage viewers included "The Untouchables," starring Robert Stack as FBI agent Eliot Ness and "Mission Impossible," with Robert Graves running a high-tech spy ring. Stack continues to be seen regularly today on TV, while "Rawhide" star Clint Eastwood has become an international movie star and a talented director.

Lucille Ball was hugely popular in The Lucy Show, *which was screened throughout the fifties and sixties. Alongside Vivian Vance, she always played a brainless but lovable character whose husband was forever having to rescue from some escapade and return her to the comfortable safety of her kitchen.*

How powerful was television? "The medium," Canadian Marshall McLuhan said, "is the message." In other words, content no longer mattered. The only thing that mattered was the experience of hearing and seeing. He believed that a television viewer's experience was enriched as much by "The Beverly Hillbillies" as by a Shakespeare play. McLuhan's theory didn't outlast the decade, but he may have gauged it correctly when he said television was an invention as important as the first printing press.

It is important to remember that, during the sixties, there were only three commercial television stations, even in many large markets. There were hints of the coming of cable television ("Keep TV free, fight pay TV," read the marquee of a worried Chicago theater owner) but the only other option for most viewers was the public television station, National Educational Television, which was taken over by the Public Broadcasting Service in 1970. Very large markets, such as New York, Los Angeles, and Chicago, soon had Spanish-language, religious, and rerun stations. But until as late as 1970, the networks were the only three significant shows in town.

Tuning into FM

Radio took a curious turn during this time. At the start of the decade, most Americans listened to stations on the AM dial. About 150 million people a day tuned in to everything from farm prices to music to religion to "Gunsmoke," which starred chubby actor William Conrad. (Conrad's deep, heroic voice did not fit his roly-poly appearance, but he found plenty of work on television for a quarter of a century playing well-fed detectives.) With the rise of the counterculture and a teenage addiction to rock music, FM stations stole many of AM's listeners. Prior to 1965, FM had been a meeting place for America's intellectuals, educators, and classical-music lovers. Hippies, and anyone else who enjoyed rock 'n' roll, soon tuned in to FM, which was less expensive to operate, and which played more music with fewer commercials.

Popular music changed a great deal from one end of the decade to the next. In 1960, Elvis Presley shared top billing with many other white males, including Jerry Lee Lewis, Bobby Darrin, Neil Sedaka, Paul Anka, Del Shannon, and Frankie Avalon.

Martha and the Vandellas were one of many successful black all-female harmony groups to hit the music charts with their own brand of funky soul music in the sixties.

The Beach Boys.

High voices, a fast and insistent bass beat, and speedy electric guitars mark the music of The Beach Boys, a group of rockers from Hawthorne, California. The quintet started singing hit records in the mid-sixties and continues to tour occasionally today.

Originally, the Beach Boys were brothers Brian (keyboards, bass), Carl (guitar), and Dennis Wilson (drums), along with their cousin, Mike Love (lead vocals, saxophone), and Al Jardine (guitar). They tried several names, from Kenny & The Cadets to Carl & The Passions before realizing that not everyone rode surfboards, drove hot rods, or lived near the beach — but everyone wanted to!

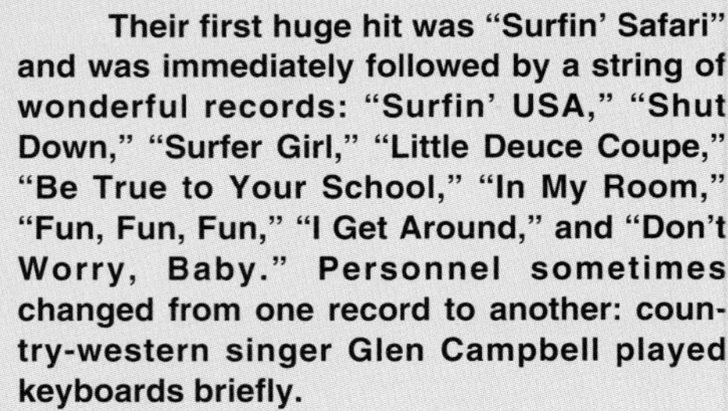

Their first huge hit was "Surfin' Safari" and was immediately followed by a string of wonderful records: "Surfin' USA," "Shut Down," "Surfer Girl," "Little Deuce Coupe," "Be True to Your School," "In My Room," "Fun, Fun, Fun," "I Get Around," and "Don't Worry, Baby." Personnel sometimes changed from one record to another: country-western singer Glen Campbell played keyboards briefly.

Brian Wilson, who wrote many of the songs, quit touring with the band in 1964. Although he continued to produce their music, he did not return to The Beach Boys traveling lineup until 1983.

Instrumentals could be popular, with "Theme From a Summer Place," by Percy Faith and "Wonderland by Night," by a German dance band, the themes of senior proms all across the country in 1960. The following year, Henry Mancini's dreamy "Moon River" took the high school formal dances by storm. Grammy Awards continued to be won by balladeers like Frank Sinatra until as late as 1966.

The early sixties saw the emergence of several influences on popular music. All-female groups, most of them black, with names like the Shirelles, the Ronettes, and Martha and the Vandellas, began cranking out hits, many of them on Detroit's Motown label. Berry Gordy, a onetime auto assembler, put together an incredible number of female rock 'n' roll groups, including the silky-voiced trio known as the Supremes, led by Diana Ross. Gordy's discoveries, such as Aretha Franklin and Gladys Knight, had learned to use their soaring voices in the choirs of African-American churches. Gordy was equally successful with male entertainers. Stars such as Smoky Robinson, Junior Walker, the Four Tops, and the Temptations made black music popular with all young people. With a string of hits in the 1960s, James Brown remains second only to Elvis Presley in the number of songs a single entertainer has had on the popular music charts.

The early sixties also saw the emergence of a national dance craze known as the twist. A song by that name was made famous in 1961 by Chubby Checker, a frequent guest on Dick Clark's "American Bandstand." Americans everywhere were twisting to "The Twist" and to hits like "Twist and Shout" and "The Peppermint Twist" by black and white entertainers alike.

As African-Americans emerged from the segregated past, so did their music. Many black southern musicians traveled to Chicago to record songs that had echoed for years across the Mississippi River. The music of Bo Diddley, John Lee Hooker, Howlin' Wolf, B.B. King, and Muddy Waters was to influence everyone from The Rolling Stones in England to Creedence Clearwater Revival in California and Z.Z. Top in Texas.

Yet rock music underwent a more radical change shortly after the middle of the decade. Counterculture musicians, many fueled by drugs, played blaring guitars and thundering drums to wild vocals. They used music created by African-Americans as a point of departure, ripping songs apart and reassembling them in ways not before imagined. British talent capable of producing "acid (drug) rock" included Cream,

Bob Dylan.

"The poet laureate of the folk revival" also was the top songwriter of the decade. Bob Dylan began life as Robert Zimmerman, the son of a hardware store owner in Hibbing, Minnesota. Dylan studied 1930s folksingers such as Woody Guthrie and taught himself how to play a Sears Roebuck electric guitar, as well as the harmonica, autoharp, and piano. When he was eighteen, he hit the road as a musician, entertaining in and around the University of Minnesota in Minneapolis.

Dylan went east to New York's Greenwich Village in 1961. A year later, his first album came out. By the middle of the decade, his music captured the feelings of millions of college age kids — against the war in Vietnam, and all other wars, for that matter. He also sang against nuclear weapons and excessive capitalism as well as more familiar themes such as lost love.

His early song titles said a lot about his music. "Masters of War," "Blowin' in the Wind," "The Times They Are A-Changin'," "A Hard Rain's A-Gonna Fall," "Talking World War III Blues," "Oxford [Mississippi] Town" — this was Dylan at his most socially conscious. He stayed ahead of his critics and fans by switching to folk-rock, surviving a storm of protest by purists when he brought electric guitars, thundering speakers, and the big rock beat to his meaningful music.

Dylan became a constantly moving target, producing a country album, cranking out pro-drug lyrics, studying Christianity and then Judaism (the religion of his parents), and telling *Rolling Stone* magazine in 1984 that politics was "an instrument of the devil." Born with a modest voice of narrow range, he nevertheless became as famous as any musician, politician, or protester in the decade's history.

Bob Dylan, on tour with fellow American folksinger, Joan Baez, in 1965.

The Beatles. (1961-1970)

There seemed to be a musical void in America in the mid-1960s, and The Beatles more than filled it. Everyone was used to Elvis Presley, folk music wasn't quite rowdy enough, and there appeared to be room for something besides the admittedly wonderful black voices that kept coming from Motown Records in Detroit. The Beatles offered volume, memorable melodies and lyrics, and albums with not one or two but several hits on each of them.

Smart suits and "mop-top" haircuts were all part of the image for The Beatles in the sixties. Here they are introduced to an American audience on the Ed Sullivan Show.

All four Beatles — Paul McCartney, John Lennon, George Harrison, and Ringo Starr — were excellent musicians who grew up in Liverpool, an industrial town on the English coast. McCartney and Lennon were also superior songwriters. They weren't especially political, preferring to poke fun rather than insult the Establishment. By 1967, they were into a drug phase, which was followed by songs about Eastern religions and mysticism.

They also were wildly popular all over the world. Virtually every teenage girl had her own favorite among the Fab Four. Even adults sensed the fun and joy in their music. Equally important, they helped other British groups export a variety of types of rock 'n' roll, from the dangerous sounds of The Rolling Stones to Cream's acid rock.

John Lennon was so confident of their success that he told a reporter in 1966, "We're more popular than Jesus now." One result of this comment was a number of record burnings in the United States by members of fundamentalist religions. McCartney and Lennon also were arrested on minor drug charges at different times. The group finally broke up in 1970.

Iron Butterfly, and Led Zeppelin.

If a single musician could be used to symbolize the 1960s, that musician would have to be Bob Dylan. A skinny kid from the frozen wilds of north Minnesota, Dylan was born Robert Zimmerman, the son of a hardware store owner. He learned to play a guitar and harmonica, then hit the road with a head full of his own folk songs, delivered in a voice that was sincere but not very tuneful.

More popular than Dylan worldwide and, some said, more popular than Elvis Presley in his prime, were the British group, The Beatles. They played pleasant, conventional rock 'n' roll until 1967, when albums such as "Sgt. Pepper's Lonely Hearts Club Band" showed that their music had taken an acid-rock turn. Lyrics became more critical of the dominant culture, the songs more heavily produced, and The Beatles narrowed their audience to precocious preteens, teenagers, and young adults. But in doing so, they became much more popular with this new audience. John Lennon, Paul McCartney, George Harrison, and Ringo Starr split up at decade's end, with Lennon and McCartney emerging as superstars in their own right.

Going to the Movies

Top movies during the 1960s were almost always in color. They included *The Sound of Music*, starring Julie Andrews, released in 1965; *Lawrence of Arabia*, starring Peter O'Toole, released in 1962; and *My Fair Lady*, with Rex Harrison, released in 1964. Perhaps because politics were in the air and people were taking sides, several major movies had political themes. The most notorious also had the longest title: *Dr Strangelove, or How I Learned to Stop Worrying and Love the Bomb.*

Stanley Kubrick directed *Dr. Strangelove*, a black and white movie released in 1964, which starred George C. Scott, Peter Sellers, and Sterling Hayden. The movie was a satire about the dangers of U.S. and Soviet atomic weapons. The film featured everything from the death by machine-gun fire of a Coca-Cola dispenser to the pilot of an American plane riding an atomic bomb into its Soviet target. *Dr. Strangelove* made audiences howl. Only hours later did moviegoers realize that they had been laughing at the futility of the arms race.

The Graduate, released in 1968, starred Dustin Hoffman and told of the lack of communication between young adults and their parents. College students, who were avid moviegoers, made this and other films with similar themes box-office hits. Another smash, the 1970 movie, *Patton*, was even more disturbing. George C. Scott played the World War II general in such a way that audiences wanted to like a man whose only real pleasure was war. The film carried a powerful antiwar message and was capped by Scott's refusal to accept an Oscar for best actor, because, as he put it, "Life is not a race. And because it is not a race, I don't consider myself in

The Sound of Music, *starring Julie Andrews, was one of the most popular family movies ever made.*

Audrey Hepburn. (1929-1993)

If teenage boys in the early 1960s wanted to be Elvis Presley or James Dean, girls longed to be Sandra Dee or Audrey Hepburn. Hepburn, born in Brussels, Belgium, of well-to-do parents, studied music and ballet in the Netherlands before appearing on the London stage immediately after World War II.

She caught the eye of television and motion-picture people and played very successfully in her first American film, *Roman Holiday,* in 1953. The role earned her an Oscar as best actress. Films that followed included *Sabrina Fair, War and Peace*, and *Love in the Afternoon*. She also triumphed on the New York stage as *Gigi.*

Small and very slim, with sharp but pleasant features, Hepburn played roles of innocence with just enough worldliness to get the best of whichever leading man was cast opposite her. Her most popular film, *Breakfast at Tiffany's* in 1960, saw her play a whimsical woman who made a New York City apartment building a fun and exciting place. She offered a snappy, intriguing contrast to stars such as Marilyn Monroe.

After that came several serious roles, including *The Children's Hour* and *Wait Until Dark.* Cast opposite Shirley MacLaine in *The Children's Hour*, Hepburn played a teacher who is unaware of the attraction of another woman for her. There also were more lighthearted films during the sixties, including *Charade, My Fair Lady, Paris When it Sizzles*, and *Two for the Road*. The roles she played consistently showed a young and single woman getting along well as an individual in the modern world.

competition with my fellow actors." *Patton* was Richard M. Nixon's favorite movie; he is said to have watched it repeatedly.

If movies were becoming more political, they also were showing more sex. The best Academy Award-winning picture of 1969 was *Midnight Cowboy*, about a handsome drifter who befriends a physically handicapped hustler in New York City. The film included heterosexual and homosexual themes and was rated X (adults aged seventeen and over only). Equally shocking, if less sexual, was the popular 1967 movie, *Bonnie and Clyde*. This film starred Warren Beatty and Faye Dunaway as fictionalized versions of 1930s outlaws. It troubled moviegoers by making them laugh one minute and turn away from scenes of gore and violence the next.

Moviegoers needed an occasional intermission from all of the heavy messages. One of the most popular family movies of all time, *The Sound of Music*, was released in 1965. Starring Julie Andrews, it told the story of an Austrian family who dodged Nazis during World War II, singing its way to freedom and success. Young people went to lighthearted films such as The Beatles' *A Hard Day's Night* or to any of a dozen old, black and white films that starred Humphrey Bogart. In films such as *Casablanca* and *The Big Sleep*, Bogey often played a tough guy, often a down-at-the-heels detective who, beneath all of his cynicism, always did the most honorable and courageous thing he could. While teens and college students were being entertained, their little brothers and sisters were enjoying *Mary Poppins*, *101 Dalmatians*, or a number of other movies from the famed cartoonist, Walt Disney.

The Arts Take Center Stage

President and Mrs. Kennedy were very receptive to a range of performing artists — they had Pablo Casals perform at the White House. Americans who had supported Jack Kennedy opened their minds to classical music, dance, theater, and poetry. They advocated partial government funding of the arts. For most of the decade, promising dance groups, theaters, and performers could submit requests for grants of government money and reasonably expect that they would be helped. Opera companies formed in places such as Anchorage and Honolulu, and symphony orchestras with big budgets could be found in about 100 different cities.

Drama and dramatists moved to the forefront of the arts. In addition to such well-known playwrights as Tennessee Williams and Archibald McLeish, Edward Albee (*A Delicate Balance*, 1967) and Frank Gilroy (*The Subject Was Roses*, 1965) took center stage. Classic plays such as Tennessee Williams' *A Streetcar Named Desire* were performed by college and amateur theater groups to the point where heroine Blanche DuBois was quoted by everyday people.

Unconventional theater also grew in popularity, usually beginning off Broadway and, because there was a craving for the unusual, sometimes made it big. *Hair*, the tribal-love rock musical, was an immense hit, with 1,750 Broadway performances. Other controversial or unusual plays that ran for months or even years included *Oh! Calcutta*, *Old Glory*, and *Dutchman*. Nudity, racial tension, and politics were common stage themes.

In literature, sexual expression reached the point where anything the mind could conceive could be found between book covers. Many previously censored books such as *Lady Chatterley's Lover* by D.H. Lawrence and *Tropic of Cancer* by Henry Miller became widely available in less expensive paperback versions. Novels that featured homosexuals, such as James Baldwin's *Another Country*, were not only read by middle America but were studied by college literature majors. Ken Kesey's *One Flew over the Cuckoo's Nest* and Joseph Heller's *Catch 22* both portrayed as heroes people their authors saw as victims of an inhumane, insane, and increasingly authoritarian society.

The rock musical Hair, *which embraced the ideals and lifestyle of the hippie movement, shocked audiences with its unashamed on-stage nudity when the show first opened, but was destined to become a long running hit on Broadway.*

Harper Lee.

The daughter of a lawyer, Harper Lee was born in Monroeville, Alabama. She attended college and then studied law at the University of Alabama before spending a year as a student at Oxford University in England.

Lee returned to the United States and worked as an airline reservation clerk for Eastern Air Lines and British Overseas Airways in New York City. Her spare time was spent writing; she was a contributor to *Vogue* magazine. The book that made her famous, *To Kill a Mockingbird*, was published in 1960. Awards and honors included the Pulitzer Prize in 1961, an Alabama Library Association award, a Book-of-the-Month Club alternate selection, and a Brotherhood Award of the National Conference of Christians and Jews.

The book is narrated by a six-year-old southern girl whose father, an attorney, defends a black man accused of the rape of a white woman. The book is tough, tender, sentimental, funny, and sad, moving back and forth among the major characters. A critic said, "Miss Lee does so well what so many American writers do appallingly: she paints a true and lively picture of life in an American small town." Lee considered the book to be a simple love story.

The author, who is related to General Robert E. Lee, writes slowly from noon until evening, completing only a page or two each day. She considers the law, with its emphasis on logical thought, a good background for a writer. *To Kill a Mockingbird* was translated into ten languages and was made into a very successful movie that starred actor Gregory Peck as the crusading lawyer.

Miss Lee is significant for what she was as much as for what she has written. A white Republican, she tried to show that most white people in the United States in the early sixties wanted democracy and justice for everyone, black as well as white. She enjoys writing about the South, she once told an interviewer, because small towns there are the last refuge of the true eccentric.

Meanwhile Norman Mailer, Tom Wolfe, and Truman Capote blurred the distinction between fact and fiction, and postmodern writers like John Barth challenged the very sanctity of language itself. Yet the only American to win the Nobel Prize for literature during the decade was John Steinbeck, whose roots could be traced to the 1930s.

Art Goes "Pop"

The line between high culture and popular culture was rubbed raw by such "pop artists" as Roy Lichtenstein, Robert Rauschenberg, and a strange fellow named Andy Warhol. An advertising artist, Warhol began to mass-produce silk-screen renditions of everyday items like cans of Campbell's Soup. Pop art, as it came to be called, was Warhol's attempt to eliminate all artistic individuality. The products, which were eventually turned out in a loft called The Factory, captured the public imagination in a big way.

Roy Lichtenstein incorporated into his paintings frames from his favorite comic strips. His colors were bold and simple and he even included

(Left) Commercial illustrator Andy Warhol became the best-known pop artist with his Campbell's Soup cans, and went on to become famous for his outrageous lifestyle, his films, and a series of silk screen portraits of movie star Marilyn Monroe.

words like "blam" and "pow" as part of the painting. Robert Rauschenberg went one step further by incorporating actual objects into his paintings. His composition *Bed* included a real quilt and pillow.

Silly as much of it seems now, pop art added to the mystique that was the 1960s.

So did clothing. For the first time in anyone's memory, wealthy, international "beautiful people" were copying clothing crazes of middle-class kids from the United States and especially Britain. Multimillionaires and their friends could be found combing Army and Navy surplus stores for the latest in wearables. For men and women alike colors were at the most unrestrained. Men wore turtlenecks for both formal and casual occasions. Shirts were striped or boldly colored with spread collars and French cuffs. Shoes were of soft leather with square toes.

In the Car, *1963, by Roy Lichtenstein. Lichtenstein said that many modern artists could get away with "hanging a wet paint rag."*

Andy Warhol. (1927-1987)

When Andy Warhol couldn't keep up with the demand for his paintings of Campbell's Soup cans, he began producing them as silk screens. When that proved even more popular, he hired friends to make the silk screens. By creating thousands of identical pieces of art on an assembly-line basis in a loft in New York he called The Factory, the artist was proving that the individuality of the artist could be totally eliminated.

Warhol may not have been the first pop artist, but he was by far the best known. The Pennsylvania native worked in advertising for several years before cranking out his products. Besides soup cans, he created likenesses in wild colors of familiar people such as Marilyn Monroe and Elvis Presley, plus familiar objects such as Brillo pad boxes.

The artist, whose real name was Warhola, was equally interesting as a film maker. His lone commercial success was *Chelsea Girls* (1967), which paid for such other efforts as *Blue Movie* and *From A to B and Back Again*. Like his art, Warhol's movies featured his friends. They ranged from such stars as Viva, and Ultra Violet, to the modestly named Ingrid Superstar.

Despite his far-out products and productions, Warhol lived with his mother and attended church every Sunday. He was never seen without sunglasses, and he virtually always dressed in black. The line for which he will be remembered is this: "In the future, everybody will be world-famous for at least fifteen minutes." Warhol meant that, with the electronic media everywhere, you're bound to turn up on nightly news, on the radio, or in the movies sooner or later. His phrase today is used to spot people who want to be stars but will probably only be celebrities for a very short time.

Like too many people during the decade, Warhol was shot. His assailant was a bit player in one of his movies, Valerie Solanos. She told police she did it for the cause of feminism. Warhol survived not only the gunshot but the sixties, dying of natural causes in 1987.

Andy Warhol, at an exhibition of his works in the Whitney Museum, 1971, is accompanied by (left) transvestite, Candy Darling, and (right) Ultra Violet.

The British model Twiggy arrived in New York in March, 1967, to show off the latest in miniskirts, boots, and pin-striped jumpsuits, all with bold, contrasting colors. The maxi coat was worn over the miniskirt and stockings were virtually replaced by tights.

Carnaby Street, a fashionable area of London, produced miniskirts and related items that were snapped up by the young and then by the not-so-young. As the decade ended, the only surefire fashion tip was this: the stranger and more idiosyncratic you appeared, the more attention you attracted and the better you felt.

(Right) So long as it was floral, it was high fashion in the sixties, when "flower power" was all the rage and bright flowery patterns appeared on every kind of garment. This cotton jacket was advertised as the latest thing in 1969.

CHAPTER 10
Summary of the Decade

The sixties were a time of momentous change, of radical social movements, of sweeping legislation which brought government closer to the lives of every American. There were incredible achievements in space, medical, and other technologies. People began to pay much more attention to their health, the environment, and public safety.

The sixties also marked the end of the consensus view, where the majority of people never questioned the status quo. In politics and the wider society, an idealism challenged the materialistic values and spirit of conformity of the fifties in a way that changed the whole American way of life for years to come.

Violence and Civil Unrest

The sixties was a most violent decade. It saw four major assassinations — a president, a presidential candidate and two of the greatest leaders that the black civil rights movement has ever seen. There were riots, rising urban violence and crime, police violence, and a growing fascination with violence on TV, in books, and at the movies. Meanwhile, the nation was engaged in a violent

> *"Violence is necessary. It is as American as cherry pie."*
>
> H. Rap Brown

A decade of violence and protest — a peace demonstrator taunts military police during an antiwar protest in front of the Pentagon in 1967.

and, many thought, immoral war on the other side of the world.

It was the decade when youth found its voice and its place as the conscience of the nation and irritant to many of its politicians. These feelings were expressed in the massive antiwar demonstrations, political activities on college campuses, and radical changes in dress and grooming. Drug use, especially of marijuana and LSD, increased. Pop music continued to outrage the older generation but now also turned its attention to criticizing politicians and the "Establishment."

It was the decade when blacks, and their white supporters, finally sat together at segregated lunch counters; they boycotted segregated buses, and organized massive demonstrations to publicize the cause of black civil rights. Before the law at least, the rights for which the nation had struggled 100 years before had at last been won.

Women, too, began to recognize that there was more to life than running a home and raising children. The Pill gave women more control over their bodies and families more control over their lives.

It was the decade when sex came out of the closet and sexual matters, sometimes quite literally, began to be aired in public. The oral contraceptive enhanced sexual liberation, while movies and theater began to portray subjects that had been taboo just a few years earlier.

The Spirit of the Decade

The decade had opened on a note of optimism and in a spirit of altruism because there was a young president in the White House with a cabinet of young people surrounding him. He had promised much and, although reticent at first, he may have delivered on most of his promises. His death by the assassin's bullet may have seemed to some to signal the end of the road for the widening of civil rights and social justice.

Johnson, however, seemed as committed as his predecessor to changing the face of the nation. His "Great Society" promised justice and a fair deal for all, but especially the underprivileged. But his hopes and the hopes of the nation were shot to pieces in the jungles of Southeast Asia. Or they were buried under the burning rubble of the inner cities, as radical blacks rejected what they saw as "token" adjustments in the status quo, which still left them as second-class citizens, and the attempts by whites to take over the black civil rights movement.

The Backlash

In 1968, the conservative Republican, Richard Nixon, was elected president, partly as a backlash against the anarchy into which the country seemed to be sliding. As the next decade unfolded, however, it seemed that the turmoil, violence in society and cynicism in government would continue. Pledged to bring the country together, Nixon's period in office was to be marred by more nationwide protests against the war, the humiliating withdrawal without victory of troops from Vietnam, and by the scandal and shame of Watergate.

These events had their roots in the violent and divisive decade of the sixties, a decade that continues to color our lives to this day.

KEY DATES

1960

February 1 — Four African-American college students in Greensboro, North Carolina, sit in at a Woolworth lunch counter after they are denied service.

April 21 — Congress approves a strong voting rights act.

May 1 — The Soviet Union shoots down an American U-2 spy plane, leading to the cancellation of a summit conference in Paris.

September 17 — A mob attacks the U.S. embassy in Panama over which flag to fly — the Panamanian or American.

December 15 — The United States announces its backing of a right-wing group in Laos. That group takes control of the country the following day.

1961

The Freedom Ride campaign travels to the South to monitor desegregation.

January 3 — The United States ends diplomatic relations with Cuba.

April 17 — Cuban exiles trained and paid by the United States stage an unsuccessful invasion of Cuba at the Bay of Pigs.

May 5 — Alan B. Shepard, Jr., is fired 116.5 miles into space in a Mercury capsule in the first U.S. piloted suborbital space flight.

1962

February 14 — President Kennedy orders U.S. military advisors to fire back if fired upon in Vietnam.

February 20 — John H. Glenn, Jr., becomes the first American in orbit as he circles the earth three times in the Friendship 7 space capsule.

October 1 — James Meredith is the first black student to enroll at the University of Mississippi after three thousand federal troops put down riots protesting his enrollment.

October 22 — President Kennedy reveals that the Soviet Union has begun to store offensive missiles in Cuba. The nation goes on wartime alert.

October 28 — Kennedy and Soviet Premier Nikita Khrushchev agree to a formula to end the missile crisis by having the missiles dismantled.

December — Rachel Carson's *Silent Spring* goes on sale, signaling the start of the modern environmental movement.

1963

Betty Friedan publishes *The Feminine Mystique.*

March 18 — The U.S. Supreme Court rules that criminal defendants must have legal counsel and that illegally acquired evidence cannot be used in state or federal court.

June 17 — Laws requiring the reciting of school prayers or Bible verses are ruled unconstitutional by the Supreme Court.

July 25 — A nuclear test-ban treaty is agreed upon by the United States, the Soviet Union, and Great Britain, barring all tests except under ground.

August 28 — The March on Washington is highlighted by Dr. Martin Luther King, Jr.'s "I have a dream" speech, about African-American demands for equal rights.

November 22 — John Kennedy

is shot and fatally wounded in Dallas, Texas. Lyndon Johnson is sworn in as president a few hours later.

November 24 — Jack Ruby, a Dallas nightclub owner, shoots and kills Lee Harvey Oswald, a suspect in the Kennedy assassination. The event is seen live on national television.

1964

January 9 — Panamanians riot and the country cuts off relations with the United States.

May 27 — The United States sends military planes to Laos.

June 22 — During Freedom Summer, three civil rights workers are reported missing in Mississippi. Their bodies are found in August, and arrests are made in October.

June 29 — A far-reaching civil rights bill is passed that bans discrimination in voting, jobs, public accommodations, and more.

August 7 — Congress passes the Tonkin Resolution, approving presidential action in Vietnam after North Vietnam is accused of firing on an American ship.

August 11 — Congress passes the War on Poverty bill.

September 27 — The Warren Commission decides that Lee Harvey Oswald alone was responsible for the Kennedy assassination.

1965

February — Continuous bombing of North Vietnam begins.

April 28 — U.S. troops are sent to the Dominican Republic during a civil war.

August 6 — A new federal Voting Rights Act is signed.

August 11 — Rioting begins in the Watts section of Los Angeles that results in thirty-four deaths and damage estimated at $200 million.

September 21 — A federal Water Quality Act is passed to reduce pollution.

October 3 — Immigration quotas are abolished.

December 31 — U.S. forces in Vietnam number 184,300.

1966

The National Organization for Women (NOW) is formed, with Betty Friedan as its leader.

May 1 — U.S. forces begin firing into Vietnam's neighbor, Cambodia, in pursuit of Viet Cong and North Vietnamese soldiers.

June 29 — Bombing of Hanoi, North Vietnam's capital, begins.

July 1 — President Johnson introduces Medicare, a government program to help persons sixty-five or older with medical costs.

1967

June 23 — The United States and the Soviet Union agree in Glassboro, New Jersey, not to let any crisis push them into war.

July 23 — Forty persons die, two thousand are injured, and five thousand are left homeless by black inner-city rioting in Detroit.

October 2 — Thurgood Marshall is sworn in as the first African-American on the U.S. Supreme Court.

December 31 — Some 475,000 U.S. troops are in Vietnam at year's end. In the United States, war protests increase.

1968

January 23 — North Korea seizes the *U.S.S. Pueblo*, a Navy ship with a crew of eighty-three.

January 30 — Viet Cong and North Vietnamese launch the Tet Offensive, a series of attacks up and down Vietnam.

March 31 — President Johnson curbs bombing of North Vietnam and announces that he will not seek reelection.

April 4 — Martin Luther King, Jr., is assassinated by a lone gunman in Memphis, Tennessee. Rioting consumes 125 cities.

May 10 — U.S.-North Vietnamese peace talks begin in Paris.

June 5 — Senator Robert F. Kennedy is shot to death by a lone gunman as he and his followers celebrate his victory in the California presidential primary.

August 28 — The Democratic presidential convention in Chicago is disrupted by street rioting and police violence, seen live on national television.

1969

April 1 — U.S. forces in Vietnam peak at 543,400.

July 20 — U.S. astronaut Neil A. Armstrong becomes the first human to set foot on the moon. He is accompanied by Edwin E. Aldrin, Jr.

November 15 — An estimated 250,000 antiwar activists march on Washington, D.C.

November 16 — News of the 1968 massacre of civilians in the village of My Lai, South Vietnam, becomes public knowledge.

FOR FURTHER RESEARCH

Chafe, William H. *The Road to Equality: Women Since 1962 (Young Oxford History of Women in the United States, Vol 10)*. New York: Oxford University Press, 1998.

Chenes, Beth Des. *Civil Rights Primary Sources: Primary Sources (American Civil Rights Resource Library)*. Farmington, MI: Uxl, 1999.

Denenberg, Barry. *Voices from Vietnam*. New York: Scholastic, 1997.

Dylan, Bob. *Lyrics, 1962-1985*. New York: Alfred A. Knopf, 1985.

Epstein, Dan. *The 60's: 20th Century Pop Culture*. Broomall, PA: Chelsea House, 2000.

Feinstein, Stephen. *Nineteen Sixties from the Vietnam War to Flower Power*. Springfield, NJ: Enslow, 2000.

Finkelstein, Norman H. *Thirteen Days/Ninety Miles: The Cuban Missile Crisis*. New York: Silver-Burdett, 1994.

Hadju, David. *Positively 4th Street: The Lives and Times of Joan Baez, Bob Dylan, Mimi Baez Farina, and Richard Farina*. New York: Farrar, Strauss, and Giroux, 2001.

Harding, Vincent. *We Changed the World: African Americans 1945-1970*. New York: Oxford University Press, 1997.

Kronenwetter, Michael. *America in the 1960s (World History Series)*. San Diego, CA: Lucent, 1998.

McCormick, Anita Louise. *The Vietnam Antiwar Movement in American History*. Springfield, NJ: Enslow, 2000.

Morgan, Edward P. *'60s Experience*. Philadelphia, PA: Temple University Press, 1992.

Schomp, Virginia. *Letters from the Home Front: The Vietnam War*. New York: Benchmark Books, 2001.

Westheider, James E. *Fighting on Two Fronts: African Americans and the Vietnam War*. New York: New York University Press, 1997.

Movies

Psycho, Shamley Productions, 1960.

The Apartment, Mirisch Co./United Artists, 1960.

West Side Story, United Artists/Mirisch Films/Beta Productions, 1961.

Lawrence of Arabia, Horizon Pictures/Columbia, 1962.

To Kill a Mockingbird, Universal Studios, 1963.

My Fair Lady, Warner Bros, 1964.

In the Heat of the Night, Mirisch Company/ United Artists, 1967.

Bonnie and Clyde, Warner Bros, 1967.

The Graduate, Embassy Pictures Corp./Lawrence Turnam Inc., 1967.

2001: A Space Odyssey, Metro Goldwyn Mayer, 1968.

Contemporary Music

I Can't Stop Loving You, Ray Charles, 1962.

People, Barbra Streisand, 1964.

Positively 4th Street, Bob Dylan, 1965.

My Girl, Temptations, 1965.

Somebody To Love, Jefferson Airplane, 1967.

Contemporary Literature

To Kill a Mockingbird, Harper Lee, 1960.

Catch 22, Joseph Heller, 1961.

Silent Spring, Rachel Carson 1962.

Ship of Fools, Katherine Anne Porter, 1962.

One Flew Over the Cuckoo's Nest, Ken Kesey, 1962.

The Bell Jar, Sylvia Plath, 1963.

A Moveable Feast, Ernest Hemingway, 1964.

The Autobiography of Malcolm X, Malcolm X and Alex Haley, 1965.

Slaughterhouse Five, Kurt Vonnegut, 1969.

Television

1960 *Andy Griffith Show*
1960 First televised Presidential Debate, Richard Nixon and John F. Kennedy
1963 Jack Ruby kills Lee Harvey Oswald on live television
1963 Networks begin evening news broadcasts
1963 *The Fugitive*
1964 *Ed Sullivan Show*, The Beatles
1965 *Mission Impossible*
1965 *Hogan's Heroes*
1966 *Star Trek*
1968 *Mr. Rogers' Neighborhood*
1968 *Sixty Minutes*
1969 Cigarette advertising banned on television and radio
1969 *Sesame Street*
1969 First broadcast from the Moon

Websites

John F. Kennedy Library
www.jfklibrary.org

Vietnam War Internet Project
www.vwip.org/vwiphome.html

Timeline of the American Civil Rights Movement
www.wmich.edu/politics/mlk/tm.html

Page numbers in *italic* indicate picture; page numbers in **bold** indicate biography

Page numbers in *italic* indicate picture; page numbers in **bold** indicate biography

ACKNOWLEDGMENTS

The author and publishers wish to thank the following for permission to reproduce copyright material: Allsport: 984; Aquarius Library: 987, 993; The Bettmann Archive: 916, 925, 932; Black Star: 918; The Bridgeman Art Library/Roy Lichtenstein/DACS 1995: 997; Culver Pictures Inc: 911, 936, 988, 995; Peter Newark's American Pictures: 870, 879, 905, 910, 926, 944, 951, 966, 971, 976, 998 (lower); Popperfoto: 891, 923, 975, 982; Redferns: 942, 989; Springer/Bettmann Film Archive: 877, 994; Topham Picture Source: 872, 888, 898; UPI/Bettmann: *frontispiece*, 875 (both), 880, 881, 883, 884, 886, 887, 889, 892, 893, 894, 895, 899, 903, 904, 906, 908, 909, 912, 914, 919, 920, 921, 923 (lower), 924, 928, 931, 934, 935, 937, 939, 940, 941, 945, 946, 949, 952, 954, 955, 957, 958, 960, 962, 963, 964, 965, 972, 973, 974, 977, 978, 979, 981, 985, 986, 990, 991, 992, 996, 997 (upper), 998 (upper), 999. The illustrations on pages 900, 901, 947, and 969 are by Rafi Mohammed.

Glen Burnie H. S. Media Center